Lonely ● planet

POCKET

LISBON

TOP EXPERIENCES • LOCAL LIFE

T0021594

SANDRA HENRIQUES &
JOANA TABORDA

Contents

Plan Your Trip   4

Mosteiro dos Jerónimos (p96)
JEANLUCICHARD/SHUTTERSTOCK ©

Explore Lisbon 35

Worth a Trip

Survival Guide 145

Special Features

Welcome to Lisbon

A roller-coaster city of seven hills, crowned by a medieval-style castle and washed in an artist's pure light, Lisbon is cinematically beautiful and historically compelling. This is a capital city of big skies and bigger vistas; of clattering trams and Willy Wonka–like elevators; of melancholic fado songs and live-to-party nightlife. Edge, charisma and postcard good looks – Lisbon has the lot.

Miradouro de Santa Luzia (p81)

Lisbon's Top Experiences

Admire Unesco-listed Manueline masterpiece, Mosteiro dos Jerónimos (p96)

BERNARD BARROSO/SHUTTERSTOCK ©

Journey through Lisbon's old neighbour-hoods aboard Tram 28 (p74)

See Lisbon from hilltop Castelo de São Jorge (p78)

Virtually dive into Lisbon's top aquarium, the Oceanário (p112)

MARTIN THOMAS PHOTOGRAPHY/ALAMY STOCK PHOTO ©

GUAXINIM/SHUTTERSTOCK ©

Stroll through riverside Praça do Comércio (p58)

Check out Lisbon's largest art collection at Museu Calouste Gulbenkian (p120)

IAN G DAGNALL/ALAMY STOCK PHOTO ©

TICH/IR/SHUTTERSTOCK ©

Visit Convento do Carmo, a roofless pre-earthquake convent (p38)

Visit Museu Nacional de Arte Antiga, Lisbon's oldest art museum (p132)

ZABOTNOVA INNA/SHUTTERSTOCK ©

STOCKPHOTOSART/SHUTTERSTOCK ©

See a private contemporary-art collection at Museu Coleção Berardo (p98)

Learn about azulejos (hand-painted tiles) at Museu Nacional do Azulejo (p92)

JONATHAN STOKES/LONELY PLANET ©

©FUNDAÇÃO MILLENNIUM BCP/ATELIER BRUECKNER GMBH – GIOVANNI EMILIO GALANELLO

Uncover Lisbon's 2500-year-old history at Núcleo Arqueológico da Rua dos Correeiros (p60)

Dining Out

ANNA_PUSTYNNIKOVA/SHUTTERSTOCK ©

While classics like bacalhau (dried salt-cod) and pastéis de nata (custard tarts) never go out of fashion, the Portuguese capital has raised the bar, with creative chefs looking towards Brazil, France, India and the Med for inspiration. Restaurants have popped up in the most unlikely places, from convents to former fish-tackle stores.

Tasca Charm

Crowded tables, an inviting buzz and trusted menus with robust Portuguese dishes like *açorda* (bread and shellfish stew) define *tascas*, Lisbon's family-run, cheap-as-chips eateries. Find an equally local scene and great value specials at *churrasqueiras* (grill houses).

Fine Dining

Simplicity, pristine ingredients and creativity mark Lisbon's gourmet scene. Contemporary chefs have put the Portuguese capital on the gastro map with ingredient-focused tasting menus, often putting a spin on comfort foods like slow-cooked suckling pig and *bacalhau*.

Pastelarias & Cafes

Sweet tooth? One visit to Lisbon's *pastelarias* (pastry shops) and you'll be hooked, we swear. Perhaps by the *pastéis de nata* (caramelised custard tarts that crumble just so; pictured above left); perhaps by the sumptuous gilt and stucco surrounds of old-world cafes; perhaps by the new-generation bakeries doing a brisk trade in French patisserie.

Best Gourmet

Alma Michelin-starred Henrique Sá Pessoa's flagship Portuguese kitchen. (p47)

Bairro do Avillez Celebrated chef José Avillez' culinary 'neighbourhood' is one-stop satisfaction for foodies. (p46)

Best Tascas & Tabernas

Tasca Zé dos Cornos A family-run favourite in Mouraria serving delectable Portuguese classics. (p86)

SUEDDEUTSCHE ZEITUNG PHOTO/ALAMY STOCK PHOTO ©

Ti-Natércia Moody Alfama gem featuring 'Aunt' Natércia's home-cooked recipes. (p87)

Best for Romance

Flor da Laranja Cosy and romantic Moroccan in Bairro Alto. (p47)

Vicente by Carnalentejana Atmospheric space serving delicacies from the Alentejo. (p46)

Best Bistros

Santa Clara dos Cogume-los A slice of vintage cool in a former market hall, with a mushroom-focused menu. (p87)

Clube de Jornalistas Pared-down elegance in an

18th-century house opening onto a tree-shaded court-yard. (p138)

Best Tapas & Small Plates

Pharmacia Appetising tapas and pharmaceutical fun in Lisbon's apothecary museum. (p47)

Os Tibetanos Lisbon's oldest vegetarian restaurant

at a Tibetan Buddhism school. (p127)

Best Old-School Pastelarias

Versailles Rather grand 1930s patisserie frequented for cream cakes and gossip. (p125; pictured above right)

Confeitaria Nacional A legendary spot in the heart of the Baixa. (p63)

Top Tips

Couvert, the bread, olives and other good-ies automatically brought to the table as appetisers, costs. You pay for what you eat, but it's fine to send it away if you don't want it.

Bar Open

As one local put it, Lisbon is Europe's Havana, with its decadence, brightly coloured buildings and party-loving vibe. And whether you're toasting new friendships in Bairro Alto's narrow lanes, rocking to gigs in Cais do Sodré or sipping ginjinha (cherry liqueur) around Rossio at dusk, you can't help but be swept along by the festive spirit.

Nightlife Districts

Take the lead of locals and begin an evening in front of a cubby-hole *ginjinha* bar around Rossio. In the mood for fado? Gravitate towards the medina-like Alfama for the real deal in softly lit, family-run clubs. Bairro Alto is one big street party and bar-hopping after midnight is the way to go. Similarly open-minded, bohemian and oblivious to sleep is sleazy-turned-trendy Cais do Sodré, with a growing crop of bordello-chic bars and all-night clubs. For a more low-key, gay-friendly vibe in cocktail bars and en-vogue cafes, swing north to Príncipe Real. Edging west of the centre, industrial-cool bars and clubs draw crowds to the riverside in Alcântara.

Best Cocktails

Pavilhão Chinês Lovely elixirs served up in a wacky wonderland setting. (p49)

Foxtrot Unapologetically art-nouveau bar chock-full of atmospheric kitsch and no shortage of creative cocktails. (p139)

Red Frog Bespoke cocktails and classy ambience in a handsomely designed speakeasy. (p128)

Best Wine Bars

ViniPortugal Sample the best of Portuguese wine at this quiet wine bar and shop by Praça do Comércio. (p59)

Ressaca Tropical Local and international natural wines, plus traditional drinks. (p48)

Best Rooftops

Park Lisbon's trendiest rooftop bar. (p48)

Memmo Alfama Stupendous views are offered at this boutique hotel bar. (p88)

CKTRAVELS.COM/SHUTTERSTOCK ©

TOPO Martim Moniz An artsy-leaning lounge with ridiculous castle views. (p69)

Sky Bar Drink in a panorama of Lisbon from this upscale rooftop along Avenida da Liberdade. (p128; pictured above)

Best Craft Beers

Quimera Brewpub One-of-a-kind beers, including offerings from local brewers. (p140)

Duque Brewpub Featuring 12 taps of Portuguese-only *cerveja artesanal* (craft beer) on an atmospheric Chiado staircase. (p49)

Outro Lado Easy-going Alfama choice leaning on Portuguese and Belgian brews. (p88)

Crafty Corner Laid-back Alfama bar with occasional live music, light meals, and 12 taps of Portuguese craft beer. (p88)

Best Live Music

Mesa de Frades Magical fado in a tiny former chapel. (p89)

A Tasca do Chico A fado favourite in Bairro Alto, with the occasional drop-in taxi driver humming a few bars. (p51)

Damas Graça's eclectic alternative concert hall. (p91)

Zé dos Bois Live music and experimental performing arts venue. (p51)

Senhor Fado An intimate and atmospheric fado spot in the heart of the Alfama. (p89)

Best Clubs

Lux-Frágil One of Europe's best megaclubs; a gay-friendly temple of dance alongside the Rio Tejo. (p88)

Discoteca Jamaica Welcoming hotspot for boogying to some reggae. (p50)

Treasure Hunt

Grid-like Bairro Alto attracts vinyl lovers and vintage devotees to its cluster of late-opening boutiques. Elegant Chiado is the go-to place for high-street and couture shopping, to the backbeat of buskers. Alfama, Baixa and Rossio have frozen-in-time stores dealing exclusively in buttons and gloves, tawny port and tinned fish.

SVETLANASF/SHUTERSTOCK ©

Gift Ideas

While there's plenty of tourist tat to be found (particularly in Baixa), Portugal does offer unique wares worth seeking out, such as cork products, *azulejos* (tiles) and quality Portuguese wines. Other things to look out for include bath products from Claus Porto, wool clothing from Loja do Burel, and beautifully wrapped tinned fish from Conserveira de Lisboa.

Cork

Portugal is famous for its cork (pictured above left), which is sustainably produced and put to myriad uses. You'll find cork wallets, handbags, sandals, notebooks, smartphone covers and even umbrellas.

Azulejos

Those exquisite ceramic tiles that adorn so many buildings around Lisbon (inside and out) make fine souvenirs. The best are hand-painted with unique designs you won't find elsewhere.

Wine

You can pick up some great wines in Portugal, often sold at a fraction of the price you'd pay in your home country. Look for reds from the Alentejo, the Douro and the Dão; semi-sparkling *vinho verde* (great on summer picnics); and one-of-a-kind fortified wines like Moscatel de Setúbal, which come from the peninsula just south of Lisbon.

Best Gifts & Souvenirs

A Vida Portuguesa Retro sanctuary with the best of Portuguese-designed products, homewares and handicrafts. (p52)

SVETLANASF/SHUTTERSTOCK ©

Apaixonarte Art gallery/shop selling locally produced decorative pieces by Portugal-based artists. (p53)

Best Speciality Stores

Cork & Company Elegant and creative wares fashioned from sustainable cork. (p53)

Best Fashion & Accessories

Kolovrat The flagship store of Lisbon's darling of fashion, Lidija Kolovrat. (p55)

Embaixada Epic 19th-century neo-Moorish palace filled with local designers. (p55)

Best Art & Design

Fábrica Sant'Ana Classic hand-painted *azulejos* factory and store in business since the 1700s. (p53)

Madalena à Janela A concept store that is a tribute to Portuguese-made art and crafts. (p91)

Best Markets

Feira da Ladra Hunt for treasures at this vibrant flea market on Campo de Santa Clara. (p91)

LX Market Popular Sunday market, with everything from food to vintage clothing. (p141)

Best Vintage

Outra Face da Lua The perfect spot to browse for a '60s shirt or a vintage prom dress. (p63)

El Dorado Plenty of whimsy and style in this Bairro Alto gem. (p53)

Best Food & Drink

Manteigaria Silva Slice of a bygone era, this shop specialises in Portuguese delicacies. (p71)

Garrafeira Nacional Long-standing specialists in Portuguese wine. (p70)

Under the Radar Lisbon

Immerse yourself in a more local scene by heading out of the city centre to untrammelled neighbourhoods far from the tourist crowds. There you'll find some of Lisbon's top ethnic eateries, speakeasy-style drinking dens, little-known overlooks and tiny parks with miraculous secrets, plus a museum on the Carnation Revolution.

Neighbourhood Exploring

Madragoa, west of Baixa, with its narrow lanes and charming restaurants, is reminiscent of Alfama, but with a fraction of the tourists. The once-derelict industrial bairro of Marvila, 4km north of Santa Apolónia, is Lisbon's up-and-coming area and the new domain of cutting-edge art galleries, hip bars and restaurants and several breweries. The leafy, grid-like Campo de Ourique, 300m west of Estrela, is a somewhat self-contained residential neighbourhood harbouring a wealth of charming pavement cafes, independent boutiques and trip-worthy bars and restaurants.

Modern History

Portugal emerged from a five-decade-long conservative dictatorship in the mid-1970s. Today, Lisbon is a vibrant, welcoming, cosmopolitan European capital city, but that dark past sometimes still hovers. While *lisboêtas* prefer to focus on the future, visitors can learn more about the history that shaped today's local culture in a state-of-the-art museum in Alfama.

Best Attractions

Miradouro Panorâmico de Monsanto Astounding city-wide panorama set in an abandoned high-society restaurant.

Campo dos Mártires da Pátria Grassy square with jacaranda trees, a duck pond, cafe and a miracle-working statue.

Museu do Aljube (www.museudoaljube.pt) This punch-in-the-gut museum (pictured above) in Alfama addresses Portugal's 50-year conservative dictatorship and the revolution that ended it.

Best Restaurants

Mezze (www.mezze.pt) Hummus heaven at this heartwarming Syrian refugee success story.

Último Porto Locals' well-kept secret, serves simple grilled fish paired with top Alentejan and Douro wines.

Mesa do Bairro (www.facebook.com/mesado bairro) Reinvents some of the most traditional Portuguese dishes in an old market setting.

Best Nightlife & Entertainment

Wine with a View (www.winewithaview.pt) Mobile bar, run from a tuk-tuk, serving glasses of Portugal's finest with views of the Tejo.

Ulysses Speakeasy Microscopic watering hole with fabulous bourbon, plus craft beers and good espresso.

Cinemateca Portuguesa (www.cinemateca.pt) Screens offbeat, art-house, world and old movies.

Tasca do Jaime Hosts authentic fado on weekends from about 4pm to 8pm.

Museums & Galleries

If Lisbon's museums and galleries have sidestepped the world spotlight, it's because the Portuguese capital whispers about its charms. Yet it has been hoarding fine art for centuries. You'll find Rodin sculptures and works by Dutch Masters, Dürer and Warhol in its uncrowded galleries, as well as fado memorabilia and geometric azulejos.

BERNARD BARROSO/SHUTTERSTOCK ©

Best Ancient & Decorative Arts

Museu Calouste Gulbenkian Treasure-trove museum with standout Egyptian artefacts, Rubens paintings and René Lalique jewellery. (p120)

Museu Nacional de Arte Antiga Peerless stash of ancient art, from Dürer originals to bejewelled chalices and Japanese screens. (p132)

Museu de Artes Decorativas Qing porcelain and French silverware in a petite 17th-century palace. (p84)

Casa-Museu Medeiros e Almeida An unsung gem of a private collection in an art-nouveau mansion. (p124)

Best Modern & Contemporary Art

Museu Coleção Berardo Warhol pop art and Picasso cubist wonders crown this outstanding collection. (p98)

Museu Calouste Gulbenkian – Coleção Moderna Homing in on 20th- and 21st-century art, with works by Hockney, Gormley and Paula Rego. Closed for renovations; due to reopen in 2023. (p124)

Museu Nacional de Arte Contemporânea do Chiado Beautifully converted convent with star pieces by Rodin and Jorge Vieira. (p44)

Best for Heritage

Museu Nacional do Azulejo Piece together 500 years of *azulejo* history. (p92)

Museu Nacional dos Coches A fantasy of fairytale coaches in the former royal riding stables. (p103; pictured above)

Museu de Marinha Circumnavigate the so-called Age of Discovery studying cannonballs and shipwreck treasures. (p105)

Museu do Oriente Be catapulted back to Portugal's first baby steps in Asia. (p136)

Museu do Fado Tune into the history of fado at this folk-music museum. (p84)

Stunning Views

JEANLUCICHARD/SHUTTERSTOCK ©

Like Rome, Lisbon sits astride seven hills, which equates to a different view for every day of the week. You might huff and puff and curse this hilly town as you climb the umpteenth cobbled calçada (stairway), but take heart: for every stairway there is a beguiling miradouro (viewpoint), for every blister a(nother) breathtaking vista.

Best Bairro Alto Miradouros

Miradouro de São Pedro de Alcântara This tree-shaded, fountain-dotted terrace has far-reaching views to the castle, the river and the Ponte 25 de Abril. (p44)

Miradouro de Santa Catarina Buskers, artists, families, couples – everyone loves the river views from Santa Catarina, especially at sundown. (p44)

Best Alfama & Graça Miradouros

Miradouro de Santa Luzia Prettily tiled terrace draped with bougainvillea and commanding long views across Alfama and Baixa. (p81)

Miradouro da Senhora do Monte They don't come higher than this pine-shaded viewpoint with photogenic perspectives of the castle. (p81; pictured above)

Best Bars & Cafes with a View

Go A Lisboa One of the city's newest rooftop bars with an eye on the view and the work-from-anywhere crowds. (p140)

Hotel Mundial Rooftop Bar Slinky white sofas, cool drinks, jazzy beats and prime views of the castle on the hillside. (p69)

Lost In A taste of India and captivating castle views await at this well-hidden, colour-charged cafe. (p47)

Le Chat This glass-fronted cafe has fine views of the Alcântara docks. (p140)

Top Tips

Want to linger? Most of the *miradouros* have kiosk cafes where you can grab a drink and snack. And don't just visit the city by day: evenings, when the city is aglow, can be just as atmospheric, if not more.

Outdoors

While Lisbon might not immediately strike you as a green city, there are well-tended parks, botanical gardens lush with palms and banyan trees, and fountain-dotted praças (squares) offering peaceful respite. For refreshing Atlantic breezes on a summer's day, head to the riverfront where you can stroll, cycle and tick off landmarks.

WIRESTOCK CREATORS/SHUTTERSTOCK ©

Beside the Sea

Bet you didn't think you'd need your bucket and spade for a trip to Lisbon. Board a train at Cais do Sodré and within 40 minutes you can be paddling in the Atlantic. Take your pick of its bays or hire a bike (free) from the station to pedal along the coast to the villa-studded resort of Estoril. Praia do Guincho, 9km northwest of Cascais, attracts surfers, kitesurfers and windsurfers to its wave-lashed beach.

Best Promenades

Ribeira das Naus A gorgeous promenade lopes along Lisbon's revamped riverfront.

Best Botanical Gardens

Jardim Garcia de Orta (www.cm-lisboa.pt/equipamentos/equipamento/info/jardim-garcia-de-orta) A riverside park nurturing colonial flora from dragon trees to frangipani.

Jardim Botânico (Botanical Garden; www.mnhnc.ulisboa.pt) Madeiran geraniums, jacarandas and a giant Moreton Bay fig tree thrive in this pocket of greenery north of Bairro Alto (pictured above).

Best Squares & Parks

Praça do Comércio Down by the river, this monumental square is the Lisbon of a million postcards.

Jardim do Príncipe Real A giant umbrella of a Mexican cedar shades this plaza, with a kids playground and open-air cafe.

For Kids

Keeping the kids amused in Lisbon is child's play. Even the everyday can be incredibly exciting: custard tarts for breakfast, rickety rides on vintage trams and Willy Wonka–like funiculars. Then there is the storybook castle, swashbuckling tales of great navigators in Belém, riverside parks and nearby beaches for free play.

MITRELIS/SHUTTERSTOCK ©

Kids in Tow

Travelling with a family can quickly add up, but Lisbon has some excellent deals. Many museums and sights offer free entry for under-12s or under-14s, while under-18s get a 50% discount. Hotels are usually well-geared to families and many will squeeze in a cot at no extra charge. The cobblestones make pushchairs hard work, but getting around on public transport is a breeze and under-fours travel free. Kids are welcome in nearly all restaurants and *meia dose* (small portions) are ideal for little appetites.

Best Hands-On Fun

Oceanário Sharks, sea otters and weird and wonderful fish splash around at Europe's second-largest aquarium. (p112)

Pavilhão do Conhecimento Physics is (finally) a bundle of laughs at this hands-on science centre. (p115)

Castelo de São Jorge A whopper of a castle with ramparts for exploring and a hair-raising history. (p78)

Best Museums

Museu de Marinha Kids can embark on their own voyage of discovery at this barge-stuffed museum. (p105)

Museu Nacional dos Coches Royal coaches that are pure Cinderella. (p103)

Museu da Marioneta Kids love the worldly puppets at this Geppetto's workshop of a museum. (p136; pictured above)

Best Outdoors

Jardim Botânico Tropical Cool off in the shade of these gardens in Belém, home to sprawling banyan trees and friendly ducks. (p104)

Jardins d'Água Splashy fun at these water gardens in Parque das Nações. (p115)

Jardim da Estrela Low-key park with duck ponds and an animal-themed playground. (p136)

Tours

GLEN BERLIN/SHUTTERSTOCK ©

Culinary Backstreets (www.culinarybackstreets. com/culinary-walks/lisbon) *Eat Portugal* co-author Célia Pedroso leads epic culinary walks through Lisbon. Try *ginjinha* (cherry liqueur) then *pastéis de nata* (custard tarts) and artisanal sheep cheese, paired with local wines.

Taste of Lisboa (www. tasteoflisboa.com) Lisbon foodie and radiant personality Filipa Valente specialises in neighbourhood-centric food tours in less touristy locales (Campo de Ourique, Mouraria).

African Lisbon Tour (www.africanlisbontour.

com) The first (and so far, the only) walking tour in Lisbon revealing the city's African history and current Black-owned businesses.

Lisbon Walker (www. lisbonwalker.com) This excellent company, with well-informed, English-speaking guides, offers themed walking tours of Lisbon.

Lisbon Cycle Tours (www.lisboncycletours.com) Brave the legendary seven hills of Lisbon on an e-bike, guided by experienced cyclists through the old neighbourhoods of Alfama and Mouraria. You'll interact with locals, enjoy fantastic

views and indulge in Portuguese delicacies.

Lisbon Bike Tour (www. lisbonbiketour.com) It's all downhill on this 3½-hour guided bike ride from Marquês de Pombal to Belém.

We Hate Tourism Tours (www.wehatetourismtours. com) Shows a unique perspective of Lisbon from inside an open-topped UMM (a Portuguese 4WD once made for the army).

HIPPOtrip (www. hippotrip.com) This fun 90-minute tour takes visitors on a land and river excursion in an amphibious vehicle that drives straight into the Rio Tejo!

LGBTIQ+

The kings and queens of Lisbon's gay and lesbian scene are the bear-leaning bars of hip Príncipe Real and the street-party atmosphere of venues around Bairro Alto's 'gay corner' at Rua da Barroca and Travessa da Espera. The big events are Lisbon Pride in June and Festival Internacional de Cinema Queer in late September.

ALEXANDER_H_SCHULZ/GETTY IMAGES ©

Best LGBT Nightlife

Bar TR3S (www.areis marcos.wix.com/tr3slisboa) Bears and friends flock to this hopping bar with outdoor seating.

Shelter Bar (www.face book.com/shelterbarlisboa) Good for craft beer, Italian-style bites and happy-hour specials.

Portas Largas (www.facebook.com/pages/Bar-Portas-Largas/181378298544382) Bairro Alto linchpin with a mishmash of gay and straight clientele.

Posh (www.facebook.com/poshclublisbon) New night-club with drag, electronic music and big stars.

Construction (www.face book.com/construction.lisbon) A top club for thirty-somethings, with pumping house music and a dark room.

Finalmente (www.final menteclub.com) Popular club with a tiny dance floor, nightly drag shows and wall-to-wall crowds.

Purex (www.facebook.com/purexclube) Unsigned Bairro Alto spot draws a lesbian and mixed crowd.

Trumps (www.trumps.pt) Lisbon's hottest younger-leaning gay club.

VALSA (www.valsa.pt) Graça's cultural centre and safe haven for independent artists and patrons of all walks of life.

Responsible Travel

Follow these tips when you're in Lisbon to leave a lighter footprint, support local and have a positive impact on local communities.

Leave a Small Footprint

Use the public transport system as much as possible.

As of July 2021, Portugal banned single-use plastic. Follow the lead and use reusable bags, cups and water bottles.

The best of Lisbon is discovered on foot, so walk (or cycle) around the city as much as possible.

Recycling bins are widely available. Glass goes in the green bin, plastic and packages in the yellow, and paper in the blue.

Tap water is safe to drink in Lisbon. Nearly 200 drinking fountains with the EPAL logo are scattered throughout the city, with safe-to-drink water for humans and pets.

Be Sustainable

Shop at markets Lisbon has dozens of daily and weekly markets selling seasonal produce, second-hand clothes and furniture, crafts, and used books. (Pictured above: Feira da Ladra, p91)

Eat at a zero-waste restaurant Check peggada. com for an updated list of zero-waste, sustainable restaurants in Lisbon (including vegan and vegetarian).

Ask to pack the leftovers Some portions at traditional, family-owned restaurants are too large for one person. Take what's left back to your hotel.

Choose hotels over short-term rentals Lisbon's housing market is in crisis. With most apartments being converted into short-term rentals, the few remaining ones have high rents that locals can't afford. Of all the short-term rentals registered in Portugal, about 25% are in Lisbon.

SEAN HSU/SHUTTERSTOCK ©

Give Back

Volunteer with a Portuguese-based social enterprise Check ongoing projects and locations at impactrip.com.

Donate two hours of your time Give back by collecting food that would go to waste and giving it to those who need it most. Find out how at re-food.org.

Support Local

Choose small businesses over large chains (international and national) when possible.

Eat locally Have your meals at small, family-owned restaurants with traditional food. Eat a great-value soup and sandwich combo at a cafe instead of at a fast-food joint.

Be selective when buying souvenirs Choose one of the *Lojas com História* (www.lojascomhistoria.pt) over shops selling mass-produced, cheap fridge magnets.

Opt for a paid tour Support a local, trained guide and choose a company with paid tours instead of one with free or tip-based experiences.

Learn More

Visit local museums like Museu do Aljube to learn more about the country's recent history.

Stay up to date on city news. Independent online newspaper *A Mensagem* (Portuguese only; www.amensagem.pt) reports daily on Lisbon.

Educate yourself about African history in Lisbon. Projects like Re-Mapping Memories (www.re-mapping.eu) are remapping Lisbon from the perspective of the colonised and the previously enslaved.

Four Perfect Days

Day 1

Start the day with a scenic ride on **tram 28E** (p74) from Praça do Comércio. Hop off to scale the ramparts of **Castelo de São Jorge** (p78; pictured), then stop for a re-energising lunch at **O Velho Eurico** (p87) before strolling the picturesque lanes of Alfama. Afterwards, grab a coffee with a view at **Largo das Portas do Sol** (p81) and get an earful of Lisbon's soulful soundtrack at the **Museu do Fado** (p84).

In the afternoon, continue on to the fortress-like **Sé de Lisboa** (p85) en route to shopping in pedestrianised Baixa. Head up to the top of **Arco da Rua Augusta** (p59) for a unique perspective of Lisbon.

Round out the evening back in lantern-lit Alfama over fado at the **Mesa de Frades** (p89).

Day 2

Head to Belém for pastries at **Antiga Confeitaria de Belém** (p105) followed by a visit to the neighbourhood's jaw-dropping sights, including **Mosteiro dos Jerónimos** (p96) and **Torre de Belém** (p103; pictured). Finish with lunch at **Feitoria** (p108).

Spend the afternoon exploring Belém's other excellent museums such as **Museu Nacional dos Coches** (p103) or **Museu de Arte, Arquitetura e Tecnologia** (p103). Afterwards, enjoy a sundowner at the riverside **À Margem** (p109).

Head back to the city centre for a fabulous meal at **100 Maneiras** (p48) and a bit of nightlife in the bar-lined streets of Bairro Alto. End the night in Cais do Sodré, with first-rate cocktails at **Pensão Amor** (p41).

Day 3

A.MAT3D/SHUTTERSTOCK ©

Spend the morning window-shopping and cafe-hopping in well-heeled Chiado. Browse unique gifts at **A Vida Portuguesa** (p52) and **Apaixonarte** (p53), then visit the evocative earthquake-scarred ruins of the **Convento do Carmo** (p38; pictured). Have lunch at the outstanding **Bairro do Avillez** (p46).

Book a walking or food tour for the afternoon, or head to the futuristic Parque das Nações, where you can take a ride on the **Teleférico** (p115) or visit the excellent **Oceanário de Lisboa** (p112).

In the evening, indulge in multicultural culinary delights at **Cantinho do Aziz** (p87). Then head out for a big night of dancing in clubbing temple **Lux-Frágil** (p88).

Day 4

A.MAT3D/SHUTTERSTOCK ©

Start the morning with a visit to the **Museu Nacional de Arte Antiga** (p132), home to one of Lisbon's best art collections. After, head over to the **Museu do Oriente** (p136) for a look at treasures from Asia. Have lunch and window-shop in the hip **LX Factory** (p141; pictured).

In the afternoon, head back to explore Baixa: take a stroll through **Praça do Comércio** (p58), go underground at **Núcleo Arqueológico da Rua dos Correeiros** (p60) and get a history lesson at **Lisbon Story Centre** (p65). Later, have a seafood feast at **Solar dos Presuntos** (p69).

If you have any energy left for cocktails, head to Bairro Alto's drinking dens like **O Bom O Mau e O Vilão** (p50) or the rooftop perch of **Park** (p48).

Need to Know

For detailed information, see Survival Guide (p145)

Currency
Euro (€)

Language
Portuguese

Visas
EU nationals need no visa. UK, US, Canadian, Australian and New Zealand visitors can stay for up to 90 days without a visa.

Money
ATMs widely available. Credit cards generally accepted, but cash preferred in some small shops and restaurants.

Mobile Phones
European and Australian mobile phones work. US visitors should check with their service provider. Cut the cost of roaming charges by buying a local SIM card.

Time
Lisbon is on GMT/UTC.

Tipping
Tip 5% to 10% if you are satisfied with the service.

Daily Budget

Budget: Less than €65

Dorm bed: €18–35

Fixed-price meal: €7–10

Lisboa Card for unlimited transport and admission discounts: €21

Midrange: €65–160

Double room in a central hotel: €60–120

Meal in a midrange restaurant: €20–30

Walking or cycling tour of the city: €15–35

Top end: More than €160

Boutique hotel room: from €120

Three-course dinner with wine: from €50

Night at a fado club: €50

Advance Planning

One month before Book excursions, top-end restaurants, theatre and opera tickets. Check the tourist office's official website (www.visitlisboa.com) for destination information.

Two weeks before Buy tickets for gigs and reserve a table in a fado club. Read Lisbon's lesser-known history on Lisboa Romana (www.lisboaromana.pt) and ReMapping Memories (www.re-mapping.eu).

A few days before Check out the upcoming Lisbon events on Agenda Cultural Lisboa (www.agendalx.pt) and bone up on your Portuguese wine knowledge on www.vinipor tugal.pt.

Arriving in Lisbon

Most international visitors arrive at Lisbon Airport (*www.ana.pt*), 8km northeast of the city. Bus connections to the centre run frequently. The quickest way to reach the centre is by taking the metro or the bus. Buses depart in front of the arrivals hall.

✈ From Lisbon Airport

Destination	Best Transport
Marquês de Pombal & Avenida da Liberdade	Metro, bus 744
Rossio & Restauradores	Metro, bus 744
Praça do Comércio	Metro
Cais do Sodré	Metro
Oriente	Metro, bus 708

Getting Around

Lisbon's public transport network is cheap and efficient. For timetables, routes and fares, see www.carris.pt and www.metrolisboa.pt.

Ⓜ Metro

To reach the airport, Oriente and Marquês de Pombal. Runs 6.30am to 1am. Single tickets €1.50.

🚋 Tram

To travel through the old quarters. Single tickets €3.

🚌 Bus

Your best bet for reaching neighbourhoods further out. Single tickets €2.

🚲 Cycling

Gira (www.gira-bicicletasdelisboa.pt) is the city's bike-sharing scheme, with 48 stations around the city (more coming soon).

Gare do Oriente (p115)

Lisbon Neighbourhoods

Marquês de Pombal, Rato & Saldanha (p119)
Top-drawer museums, pristine gardens and some of Lisbon's best restaurants lure you north.

Belém (p95)
Manueline monuments, a Unesco-listed monastery and contemporary art await in this nautical-flavoured neighbourhood by the river.

Estrela, Lapa, Alcântara (p131)
A world-class ancient-art museum, streets with low-key, leafy charm and dockside nightlife entice in these neighbourhoods.

Museu Nacional de Arte Antiga ◉

Mosteiro dos Jerónimos ◉

◉ *Museu Coleção Berardo*

Parque das Nações (p111)
This riverside district shines with outdoor art, futuristic architecture, and Europe's second-biggest aquarium.

Oceanário de Lisboa 👁

Baixa & Rossio (p57)
The city's spiritual heart captivates with its must-see sights and handsome plazas, old-school speciality shops and little *ginjinha* bars

👁 *Museu Calouste Gulbenkian*

Mouraria, Alfama & Graça (p77)
Discover fado, character-filled backstreets and high-rise viewpoints in this trio of castle-crowned neighbourhoods.

Museu Nacional do Azulejo 👁

Tram 28E
👁 *Castelo de São Jorge* 👁

Convento do Carmo 👁

👁 *Núcleo Arqueológico da Rua dos Correeiros*

Praça do Comércio 👁

Bairro Alto & Chiado (p37)
Browse boutique shops, ride vintage funiculars to *miradouros* and hit Lisbon's most happening bars in these central neighbourhoods

Explore
Lisbon

Worth a Trip 👀

Lisbon's Walking Tours 🥾

Sala dos Brasões, Palácio Nacional de Sintra (p143)
SKY SAJJAPHOT/SHUTTERSTOCK ©

Explore ◉

Bairro Alto & Chiado

Two neighbourhoods, two very different personalities. Chiado invites days spent boutique-shopping, gallery-hopping and lingering in literary cafes. Its more rakish, party-loving neighbour is Bairro Alto, a tangle of lanes harbouring dozens of shabby-chic shops, late-night bistros and hole-in-the-wall bars. Swinging south, Cais do Sodré has reinvented itself from red-light district to nightlife hub.

The Short List

○ **Mercado da Ribeira (p52)** *Overwhelming yourself in one of Europe's best gourmet food courts.*

○ **Igreja & Museu São Roque (p44)** *Admiring the dazzling interior of gold, marble and Florentine azulejos at this 16th-century Jesuit church.*

○ **Convento do Carmo & Museu Arqueológico (p38)** *Getting wowed upon entering the roofless remnants of this survivor of the 1755 earthquake.*

○ **Ascensor da Glória (p45)** *Riding this storied funicular to the viewpoint at Miradouro de São Pedro de Alcântara, one of Lisbon's most panoramic.*

Getting There & Around

Ⓜ The green and blue lines stop at Baixa-Chiado; the green line runs to Cais do Sodré.

🚋 Trams 15E and 18E stop at Cais do Sodré and tram 25E at Rua de São Paulo. Tram 28 is convenient for Santa Catarina.

🚌 Bus 758 (Cais do Sodré–Benfica) stops at the Ascensor da Glória and Príncipe Real.

Bairro Alto & Chiado Map on p42

Ascensor da Bica (p44) SILVERFOX999/SHUTTERSTOCK ©

Top Experience

Travel Back in Time at the Convento do Carmo

Soaring above Lisbon, the Convento do Carmo, founded as a convent for the Carmelite Order in 1389, was all but devoured by the 1755 earthquake. Its shattered pillars and wishbone-like arches are completely exposed to the elements. The 19th-century taste for romantic ruins meant it was never restored, and it became the archaeology museum you see today.

◎ MAP P42, F4

www.museuarqueologico
docarmo.pt

Nave

Open to the sky, the nave is scattered with evocative tombstones, statues, baptismal fonts and coats of arms. Look for the Renaissance loggia from Santarém, the Manueline window from the Mosteiro dos Jerónimos, 6th-century Hebraic funerary stelae and the baroque statue of St John Nepomucene from the old Alcântara bridge.

Main Chapel

First up in the captivating archaeology museum is the main chapel, decorated with three baroque *azulejo* (tile) panels. It shelters the tomb of Nuno Álvares Pereira, who had the convent built to trumpet Portuguese victory in the 1385 Battle of Aljubarrota, alongside the early-14th-century tomb of Fernão Sanches, vividly depicting a boar hunt.

Pre-Columbian Treasures

Aztec statues, Chimu ceramics, Inca zoomorphic pottery and a trio of mummies – one battered Egyptian and two gruesome 16th-century Peruvians – are on display in room 4. The blue-and-white *azulejos* depict scenes from the Passion of Christ.

Roman-Moorish Collection

Roman milestones, funerary stelae and sarcophagi are showcased alongside later finds like a 6th-century Visigothic belt buckle in room 2. Two pillars adorned with griffins and a lion frieze are among the medieval Moorish standouts.

Prehistoric Finds

In room 1 you can zip back to prehistoric times contemplating Palaeolithic hand axes, Neolithic pottery, Megalithic tomb objects and Chalcolithic artefacts like loom weights.

★ Top Tips

○ For the best photographs of the convent perched on the hillside, head down to Rossio.

○ In summer, Lisbon Under Stars – an immersive video recounting Portugal's history – is reflected on the convent's walls.

○ Free 30-minute guided tours run daily at 11am and 4pm in Portuguese, French, Spanish or English.

✕ Take a Break

Savour Portuguese mead, and *petiscos* (snacks/tapas) such as flamed chorizo at the medieval tavern **Trobadores** (www.facebook.com/TrobadoresBar/), a couple of minutes' stroll away.

At the back of the convent, **Carmo rooftop** (www.carmorooftop.pt) shakes and stirs cocktails on an outdoor lawn with stunning views of the Santa Justa lift and the Castelo de São Jorge.

Walking Tour 🥾

Cais do Sodré Bar Crawl

For years, riverside Cais do Sodré's backstreets were the haunt of whisky-slugging sailors craving after-dark sleaze. But in 2011 the district was upgraded from seedy to stylish. Rua Nova do Carvalho was painted pink and the sex workers were sent packing, but the edginess and decadence on which Lisbon thrives remain in this bairro (neighbourhood) that's perfect for a late-night bar crawl.

Walk Facts

Start A Tabacaria; M Cais do Sodré

End Pensão Amor; M Cais do Sodré

Length 500m; 2–3 hours

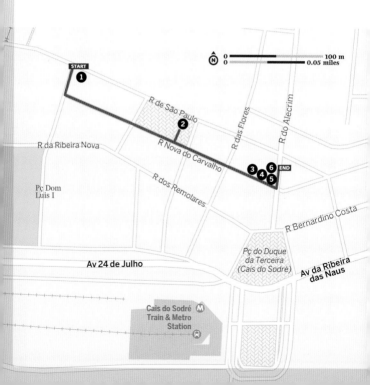

❶ Tailored Cocktails

Begin an evening in mellow fashion at the small and intimate **A Tabacaria**. The bartender creates a cocktail on the spot according to your preferences. Stay inside or enjoy it with the crowd that spills onto the pavement.

❷ Kiosk Break

Make a quick pit stop at the **Quiosque de São Paulo** (www.facebook.com/profile. php?id=100067832497577) to grab a *ginjinha* (sour-cherry liqueur) or a boozy shot of *jeropiga* (aguardiente mixed with grape must). If you're hungry you can always tuck into a *petisco* or two, courtesy of the chef from **Taberna da Rua das Flores** (p46).

❸ Tinned-Fish Tapas

Rods, hooks and nets give away the former life of tiny **Sol e Pesca** (www.facebook.com/solepesca) as a fishing-tackle shop. Cabinets are stacked with vintage-looking cans of sardines, tuna and other tinned seafood, or *conservas* as the Portuguese say. Grab a chair, order a tin or two, and accompany it with bread, olives, wine and good company.

❹ Rising Fado Stars

When it comes to fado, it can be hard to find the real deal. Well, **Povo** (www.povolisboa.com) is it. A different *fadista* (fado singer) is in residence every month, there is no stage, *petiscos* (tapas) are served, and the aim is to give young, little-known singers exposure. The fado stars of tomorrow? Hear them here first.

❺ Gigs Under the Bridge

Tucked under the arches of a bridge, the cave-like **Musicbox** (www.musicboxlisboa.com) is all about the music. This is hands down one of the city's best venues for gigs, and you rarely pay more than €15 for a ticket. Concerts cover the entire spectrum, from jazz to indie, rock, metal and DJs.

❻ Bordello Chic

If the name **Pensão Amor** (www. pensaoamor.pt) doesn't give the game away, the graffiti murals of cavorting nudes and the scarlet walls surely will. A brothel reborn as an art space, with a bordello-chic bar serving creative cocktails and a maze of rooms with velvet seats, pole bars and other secret displays. Concerts, DJs, plays and poetry recitals attract the crowds. Expect to queue at the weekend – it's worth the wait.

Bairro Alto & Chiado

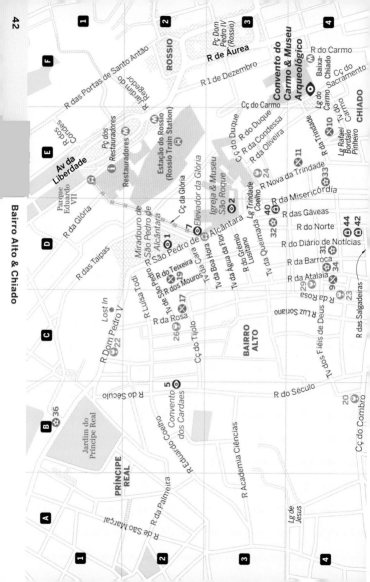

F

ROSSIO

Pç Dom Pedro IV (Rossio)

R de Áurea

R 1 de Dezembro

R das Portas de Santo Antão

R do Jardim do Regedor

Cç
des
Condes

E

Av da Liberdade

Pç dos Restauradores

Restauradores Ⓜ

Estação do Rossio (Rossio Train Station) Ⓣ

Parque Eduardo VII

R da Glória

D

R das Taipas

Miradouro de São Pedro de Alcântara

Cç da Glória

R São Pedro de Alcântara

Elevador da Glória

Ⓧ 1

7

Igreja & Museu São Roque

Ⓧ 2

Cç do Duque

R do Duque

R da Condessa

R da Oliveira

Cç do Carmo

R do Carmo

Baixa-Chiado

Cç do Sacramento

Lg do Carmo

Ⓧ 10

CHIADO

Tv do Carmo

Convento do Carmo & Museu Arqueológico

Lg Rafael Bordalo Pinheiro

R da Trindade

R Nova da Trindade

Ⓧ 11

33

R da Misericórdia

Lg Trindade Coelho 24

40

32

R das Gáveas

R do Norte

44
42

R do Diário de Notícias

31

R da Barroca

34

R da Atalaia

29

9

23

R da Rosa

R da Quimada

Tv da Queimada

Tv da Água da Flor

R do Grêmio Lusitano

R da Boa Hora

Tv da Cara

C

Lost In

R Dom Pedro V

22

R Luísa Todi

R da Rosa

26

Cç do Tijolo

R do Teixeira

19

Tv de São Pedro

Tv dos Mouros

17

BAIRRO ALTO

R Luz Soriano

Tv dos Fiéis de Deus

R das Salgadeiras

R do Século

R do Século

20

Cç do Combro

B

36

Jardim do Príncipe Real

PRÍNCIPE REAL

R do Século

Convento dos Cardaes

5

R Eduarda Coelho

Cç do Tijolo

R Academia Ciências

Lg de Jesus

A

R de São Marçal

R da Palmeira

1

2

3

4

Bairro Alto & Chiado

R Nova do Almada **5**

R Cç Nova de São Francisco

R Ivens

45 **18** **37** Kaffeehaus

R Anchieta

R Capelo

Baixa- **Chiado** **38**

Lg de São Carlos

R Paiva de Andrade

Mantegaria ●

Pç Luís de Camões

8 **15**

R da Emenda

R da Horta Seca

Lg do Barão de Quintela

Tv de Guilherme Coussel

Fábrica Coffee Roasters ●

Landeau ●

43

R das Flores

R do Alecrim

R do Atalde

R de São Paulo

R da Ribeira Nova

R de Santa Catarina

Miradouro de Santa Catarina

Tv de Santa Catarina

R Marechal Saldanha

R do Almada

Tv do Sequeiro

Tv da Bica de Duarte Belo

Ascensor da Bica **6**

28 **4** **16**

27

SANTA CATARINA

The Mill ●

Tv da Condessa do Rio

R de Santa Catarina

13

R da Boavista

Tv Alcaide

Hello, Kristof ●

41 **21**

R dos Negros

R do Poço

R Fernandes Tomás

R Gaivotas

R do Instituto Indústrial

Pç Dom Luís I

R Dom Luis I

Av 24 de Julho

Pç Dom Luís I

R de São Francisco

Lg da Academia Nacional de Belas Artes **6**

Museu Nacional de Arte Contemporânea do Chiado

R Serpa Pinto

35

3 R Vitor Cordon

R António Maria Cardoso

R do Alecrim

Tv do Alecrim

14 **12**

25

R Nova do Carvalho

R dos Remolares

Pç do Município

Pç do Município

Cç do Ferragial

39

R Bernardino Costa

Lg Corpo Santo

Pç do Duque da Terceira (Cais do Sodré)

R do Arsenal

Cais do Sodré Train & Metro Station

30

R da Cintura do Porto de Lisboa

7

8

Av da Ribeira das Naus

Av da Ribeira das Naus

Rio Tejo

For reviews see	
● Top Experiences	p38
● Sights	p44
✕ Eating	p45
✕ Drinking	p48
✕ Entertainment	p51
● Shopping	p52

200 m
0.1 miles

N

0
0

A **B** **C** **D** **E** **F**

5 **6** **7** **8**

Sights

Miradouro de São Pedro de Alcântara
VIEWPOINT

1 ◉ MAP P42, D2

Hitch a ride on vintage Ascensor da Glória from Praça dos Restauradores, or huff your way up steep Calçada da Glória to this terrific hilltop viewpoint. Fountains and Greek busts add a regal air to the surroundings, and the open-air kiosk doles out wine, beer and snacks, which you can enjoy while taking in the castle views and live music.

Igreja & Museu São Roque
CHURCH

2 ◉ MAP P42, D3

The plain facade of 16th-century Jesuit Igreja de São Roque belies its dazzling interior of gold, marble and Florentine *azulejos* – bankrolled by Brazilian riches. Its star attraction is **Capela de São João Baptista**, a lavish confection of amethyst, alabaster, lapis lazuli and Carrara marble. The **museum** adjoining the church is packed with elaborate sacred art and holy relics. (https://mais.scml.pt/museu -saoroque/)

Museu Nacional de Arte Contemporânea do Chiado
MUSEUM

3 ◉ MAP P42, E6

Art fans flock to Museu do Chiado, housed in the strikingly converted Convento de São Francisco. While the gallery's permanent collection of 19th- and 20th-century works features pieces by Rodin, Jorge Vieira and José de Almada Negreiros, you won't see them unless they have made their way into the temporary-only exhibitions. (MNAC; www.museuartecontemporanea.pt)

Miradouro de Santa Catarina
VIEWPOINT

4 ◉ MAP P42, B5

Students bashing out rhythms, pot-smoking hippies, stroller-pushing parents and loved-up couples all meet at this precipitous viewpoint in boho Santa Catarina. The views are fantastic, stretching from the river to the Ponte 25 de Abril and Cristo Rei.

Convento dos Cardaes
CONVENT

5 ◉ MAP P42, B2

The inconspicuous, graffitied white facade of this 17th-century fort-like convent contrasts with the rich blue-and-white tiles and gilded carvings of the church inside. As one of the few buildings that remained intact after the 1755 earthquake, the convent is a rare example of the Portuguese baroque style in Lisbon. Guided tours take about an hour. (www.conventodoscardaes.com)

Ascensor da Bica
FUNICULAR

6 ◉ MAP P42, C6

This funicular has been creaking arthritically up the steep, narrow

Rua da Bica de Duarte Belo since 1892. Jump aboard to save your legs and enjoy fleeting glimpses of the Rio Tejo and pastel-hued houses. (www.carris.pt/viaje/carreiras/53e-ascensor-bica)

Elevador da Glória   FUNICULAR

7 ⊙ MAP P42, D2

Lisbon's second-oldest funicular has been shuttling folk from Praça dos Restauradores to Rua São Pedro de Alcântara since 1885. Knockout views await at the top. (www.carris.pt/viaje/carreiras/51e-ascensor-gloria/)

Eating

Ao 26 – Vegan Food Project   VEGAN €

8 ✖ MAP P42, D5

So good it even lures in devout carnivores, this small, hip and bustling place offers elaborate, daily-changing chalkboard specials (eg roasted tofu with ponzu sauce and orange). There's a fixed menu of loaded seitan burgers, beet burgers and veg sandwiches on *bolo do caco* (round bread cooked on a basalt stone slab), plus Lisbon craft beer. (www.facebook.com/26veganfoodproject)

Tantura   ISRAELI €

9 ✖ MAP P42, D4

This Middle Eastern godsend started with a love story: Israeli couple Elad Bodenstein and Itamar Eliyahuo fell in love with

Portugal on their honeymoon and perceptively realised Lisbon needed hummus. A long list of hummus and shakshuka – often embellished with creative touches sourced from Romania, Poland, Iraq and Tunisia – now fills that void exceptionally. Lovely staff as well. (www.tantura.pt)

Boa-Bao   ASIAN €€

10 ✖ MAP P42, E4

The food at this trendy spot will transport you to Laos, Cambodia, Malaysia and Vietnam, but the ceramic swallows draped across the exposed brick archway (the most famous artwork of Rafael Bordalo, the artist for which the beautiful Chiado plaza is named) are undeniably Portuguese. (www.boabao.pt)

Boa-Bao

WRESTOCK CREATORS/SHUTTERSTOCK ©

Have Your Cake

Lisbon has one seriously sweet tooth and nearly every corner has a *pastelaria* (pastry shop). Housed in a revamped butter factory, **Manteigaria** (Map p42, D5; www.facebook.com/manteigaria.oficial) hits the mark with its superb *pastéis de nata* – crisp custard tarts. For flawless chocolate cake, **Landeau** (Map p42, D6; www.landeau.pt) is unrivalled.

Bairro do Avillez PORTUGUESE €€

11 🍴 MAP P42, E4

Step into this culinary venture by Portugal's most famous chef – Michelin-starred maestro José Avillez – who has set up his gastronomic dream destination: a 'neighbourhood' featuring several dining environments, including everything from a traditional tavern to a seafood-and-fish-driven food court, and an avant-garde cocktail bar. (www.bairrodoavillez.pt)

Vicente by Carnalentejana PORTUGUESE €€

12 🍴 MAP P42, D7

This sexy restaurant dishes up succulent beef and pork dishes made with ultra-premium Carnalentejana PDO-certified meat from the Alentejo, along with wines, cheeses, olive oils and other treats produced by the same artisanal farmers. In this former coal shop turned carnivore's den of decadence, the original low-slung stone walls, exposed air ducts and filament light bulbs are notably atmospheric. (www.vicente.carnalentejana.pt)

Tricky's MEDITERRANEAN €€

13 🍴 MAP P42, B6

After winning people over with her natural wine selection at the Rebel Rebel store, New Yorker Jenifer Duke set up this venture in 2022 in the party district of Cais do Sodré. Together with her Portuguese pal João Magalhães Correia, they've created a perfect combo of delicious organic food (with plenty of veggie options), rare natural wine finds and a curated soundtrack to get you dancing. (www.cometotrickys.com)

Collect GASTROPUB €€

14 🍴 MAP P42, D7

Collect is the brainchild of Mariana Barosa and João Maria Girão, two popular DJs who have been part of the city's music scene since the 1990s, and Bernardo Girão, who is in the food industry. It's the perfect spot to grab a late-night burger and a cocktail, but you can also browse through their record store upstairs. (www.collect.pt)

Taberna da Rua das Flores PORTUGUESE €€

15 🍴 MAP P42, D5

You'll have to get past the owner's unfortunate 'My way or the highway' attitude, but if you do, this tiny throwback tavern does a daily-changing, locally sourced chalkboard menu of creative small plates, all market-fresh and fantastic. Cash only. No reservations. (www.tberna.com)

Pharmacia MEDITERRANEAN €€

16 MAP P42, B5

At this wonderfully quirky restaurant in Lisbon's apothecary museum, chef Susana Felicidade (Algarvian grandmother–trained!) dispenses tasting menus and tapas singing with flavours that are both market fresh and Mediterranean influenced. Appetisers served in test tubes, cabinets brimming with pill bottles and flacons – it's all part of the pharmaceutical fun. The terrace is a great spot for cocktails. (www.chef-felicidade.pt)

Flor da Laranja MOROCCAN €€

17 🍴 MAP P42, C2

Casablanca native Rabea Esserghini runs a one-woman show at the wonderful Flor da Laranja. Service is slow, but the cosy North African ambience and delicious Moroccan cuisine more than make up for it. Top picks include dolmas, mouthwatering couscous dishes, lamb, shrimp and veggie tagines, chicken with lemon confit, and fresh berry crepes for dessert.

Alma MODERN PORTUGUESE €€€

18 🍴 MAP P42, F5

Two-Michelin–starred Henrique Sá Pessoa's flagship Alma is one of Portugal's destination restaurants and, in our humble opinion, Lisbon's best gourmet dining experience. The casual space exudes understated style amid

---

Cafe Culture

Bairro Alto and Chiado have a crop of boho-flavoured cafes good for whiling away an afternoon or evening. Elegant **Kaffeehaus** (Map p42, F5; www.kaffeehaus-lisboa.com) is a picturesque spot for coffee and Austrian fare. For drinks and light bites with knockout views, head to the Indo-chic terrace at **Lost In** (Map p42, C1; https://lostin restaurante.com/), shaded by colourful parasols.

Those more interested in high-quality espressos and pour-overs should check out Lisbon's third-wave cafes, including the Scandinavian-inspired **Hello, Kristof** (Map p42, A5; www.hello kristof.com), Aussie-Portuguese-owned **The Mill** (Map p42, A5; www. themill.pt), and **Fábrica Coffee Roasters** (Map p42, D6; www.fabrica coffeeroasters.com) with its locally roasted beans.

the original stone flooring and gorgeous hardwood tables, but it's Pessoa's outrageously good nouveau Portuguese cuisine that draws the foodie flock from far and wide. (www.almalisboa.pt)

100 Maneiras   FUSION €€€

19  MAP P42, D2

How do we love 100 Maneiras? Let us count the 100 ways... The three tasting menus (including a vegetarian option) feature 10 to 17 imaginative, delicately prepared dishes. The courses are all a surprise but include nods to the chef's Bosnian roots and a touch of Portuguese influence. Reservations are essential for the elegant and small space. (www.restaurante 100maneiras.com)

Drinking

Park   BAR

20 MAP P42, B4

If only all multistorey car parks were like this... Take the lift to the 5th floor, and head up and around to the top, which has been transformed into one of Lisbon's hippest rooftop bars, with sweeping views reaching right down to the Rio Tejo and over the bell towers of Igreja de Santa Catarina. (www.facebook.com/parklisboaofficial)

Ressaca Tropical   WINE BAR

21 MAP P42, A5

Low-intervention and natural wines are the selling point at this laid-back bar halfway between

100 Maneiras

M SOBREIRA/ALAMY STOCK PHOTO ©

Bairro Alto

For years, working-class Bairro Alto was the place to throw off your Salazar straitjacket and indulge in a little after-dark sleaze. But while sex workers no longer prowl these alleyways, the libertine lives on: graffitied slums have morphed into shabby-chic boutiques, alternative arts venues, tiny bistros, bars and clubs. It's lacklustre and as dead as a disused theatre by day, but come twilight the nocturnal hedonist rears its sleepy head. Lanterns are flicked on, shutters raised and taxi drivers hurtle through the grid of narrow lanes.

For the real spirit of Bairro Alto, take the lead of locals: move from one bar to the next as the mood and music takes you; head out onto the cobbles to toast new-found friendships with €1 beers; live for the night.

Bairro Alto and Santos. There are dozens of bottles available here, hailing anywhere from Australia, Germany, and Portugal, of course. Alongside the wines, Ressaca Tropical has other traditional drinks, such as *medronho* (moonshine) from the Alentejo or Poncha from Madeira Island. (www.ressacatropical.com)

Pavilhão Chinês   BAR

 22 MAP P42, C1

Pavilhão Chinês is an old curiosity shop of a bar with oil paintings and model Spitfires dangling from the ceiling, and cabinets brimming with glittering Venetian masks and Action Men. Play pool or bag a comfy armchair to nurse a port or an exquisitely mixed classic cocktail (from €10). Prices are higher than elsewhere, but such classy kitsch doesn't come cheap.

Tasca Mastai   BAR

 23 MAP P42, C4

This artsy, Italian-run bar-cafe is a refreshing change of pace for Bairro Alto – the long list of speciality Aperol spritzes are worth the trip (try the tart and appley Hugo, summer-drink perfection in a glass). It's a small, corner spot, with old sewing tables and tightly spun corrugated-cardboard bar stools. Bruschettas help soak up all those cocktails. (www.facebook.com/tascadomastai)

Duque Brewpub   CRAFT BEER

 24 MAP P42, E3

Lisbon's inaugural brewpub features 12 taps of Portuguese-only craft brews, a few of which are dedicated to on-site suds (under the banner of Duque), brewed in true craft-beer style: no two batches are the same. Additional taps feature invitees such as Dois Corvos, Musa and Letra. (www.duquebrewpub.com)

O Bom O Mau e O Vilão
COCKTAIL BAR

25 🚇 MAP P42, D7

'The Good, the Bad and the Ugly' is an artsy drinking den sprung from a refurbished Pombaline town house. It's divided among several rooms draped in contemporary artworks and period furnishings. DJs throw down funk, soul, acid jazz and vintage beats to an eclectic, easy-on-the-eyes crowd that is mingle friendly and more highbrow than average for the neighbourhood. (www.obomomaueovilao.pt)

Loucos & Sonhadores
BAR

26 🚇 MAP P42, C2

This smoky, bohemian drinking den feels secreted away from the heaving masses on nearby streets. With kitschy decor, free (salty) popcorn and a wide range of tunes, it's a great place for eclectic conversation in the various rooms rather than downing shots.

Musa da Bica
CRAFT BEER

27 🚇 MAP P42, B6

If you can't make it to Musa's brewery in Marvila, this offshoot near Bica is your best chance to try their freshest brews. The 15 taps are full of their iconic music-pun pours like the Eye of the Lager,

Born in the Ipa or Saison O'Connor. Grab your beer of choice and join the crowds spilling out into the streets. (www.cervejamusa.com)

Noobai Café
BAR

28 🚇 MAP P42, B5

Great views, winning cocktails (€8 to €12) and a festive crowd make Noobai a popular draw for a sundowner at Miradouro de Santa Catarina. The vibe is laid back, the music is funky jazz and the views over the Rio Tejo are magical. (www.noobaicafe.com)

Capela
BAR

29 🚇 MAP P42, D4

According to (questionable) legend, this was once a Gothic chapel, but today Capela's gospel is an experimental line-up of electronica and funky house. Get there early (before midnight) to appreciate the DJs before the crowds descend. Frescos, Renaissance-style nude murals and dusty chandeliers add a boho-chic touch. (www.facebook.com/acapelabar)

Discoteca Jamaica
CLUB

30 🚇 MAP P42, D8

Gay and straight, black and white, young and old – everyone has a soft spot for this offbeat club. It gets going at around 2am on weekends with DJs pumping out reggae, hip-hop and retro. (www.facebook.com/jamaicalisboa)

Entertainment

A Tasca do Chico
LIVE MUSIC

31 ⭐ MAP P42, D4

This crowded dive (reserve ahead), full of soccer banners and spilling over with people of all ilks, is a fado free-for-all. It's not uncommon for taxi drivers to roll up, hum a few bars, and hop right back into their cabs, speeding off into the night.

Alface Hall
LIVE MUSIC

32 ⭐ MAP P42, D3

With one wall covered in LPs and another with a vintage motorbike, there's an old-time feel to this jazz and blues bar in Bairro Alto. DJs take over Thursdays to Saturdays from 8pm. (www.facebook.com/Alface.hall.hostel.bar)

Fado in Chiado
LIVE MUSIC

33 ⭐ MAP P42, E4

Inside a small theatre, the 50-minute nightly shows here feature high-quality fado – a male and a female singer and two guitarists – and they're held early so you can grab dinner afterwards. (www.fadoinchiado.com)

Zé dos Bois
LIVE MUSIC

34 ⭐ MAP P42, D4

Focusing on tomorrow's music and performing-arts trends, this experimental venue has a graffitied courtyard and an eclectic line-up of theatre, film, visual arts and live music. (ZDB; www.zedosbois.org)

Teatro Nacional de São Carlos
THEATRE

35 ⭐ MAP P42, E5

Teatro Nacional de São Carlos is worth visiting just to see the sublime gold-and-red interior (email ahead for €8 guided tours), and it has opera, ballet and theatre seasons. The summertime **Festival ao Largo** (www.festivalaolargo.pt) features free outdoor concerts on the plaza facing the theatre. (www.saocarlos.pt)

Real Fado
LIVE MUSIC

36 ⭐ MAP P42, B1

Away from the traditional bars and restaurants, this local initiative has given a new stage to fado. Every week they take over an alternative venue in Príncipe Real, from the

Food court, Mercado da Ribeira (p52)

19th-century palace of Embaixada to an underground cistern. The shows combine revered singers with uprising talents who bring a modern touch to this traditional Portuguese music. (www.ticketline.sapo.pt/evento/real-fado-20617)

Shopping

A Vida Portuguesa

GIFTS & SOUVENIRS

37 🔒 MAP P42, F5

A flashback to the late 19th century with its high ceilings and polished cabinets, this former warehouse and perfume factory lures nostalgics with its all-Portuguese products, from retro-wrapped Tricona sardines to Claus Porto soaps, and heart-embellished Viana do Castelo embroideries to Bordalo Pinheiro porcelain swallows. There's also a location in **Intendente** (www.avidaportuguesa.com)

Loja da Burel

CLOTHING

38 🔒 MAP P42, E5

Once a clothing staple of Serra da Estrela mountain-dwelling shepherds, Burel, a Portuguese black wool, was all but left to disappear until this company single-handedly resurrected the industry, giving it a stylish makeover fit for 21st-century fashion. The colourful blankets, handbags, jackets, hats and other home decor items aren't like anything anyone has back home. (www.burelfactory.com)

Loja das Conservas

FOOD

39 🔒 MAP P42, E7

What appears to be a gallery is on closer inspection a fascinating temple to tinned fish (or *conservas* as the Portuguese say) – the result of an industry on its deathbed revived by a savvy marketing about-face and new generations of hipsters. The retro-wrapped tins, displayed along with the history of each canning factory, are artworks. (www.facebook.com/lojadasconservas)

Claus Porto

COSMETICS

40 🔒 MAP P42, D3

The amazing flagship store is in Porto, but Claus Porto, one of Portugal's most iconic brands, has its own evocative retro Lisbon boutique here as well. The painstakingly vintage art-deco and

---

Mercado da Ribeira

Doing trade in fresh fruit and veg, fish and flowers since 1892, this domed **market hall** (www.timeoutmarket.com) has been the word on everyone's lips since *Time Out* transformed half of it into a gourmet food court in 2014. Now it's Lisbon in chaotic culinary microcosm: Garrafeira Nacional wines, Café de São Bento steaks, Manteigaria Silva cold cuts and Michelin-star chef creations from Henrique Sá Pessoa.

Shop & Stroll

Chiado's well-heeled Rua do Carmo is a catwalk to posh jewellers and old-style shops like Luvaria Ulisses, while Rua Garrett is peppered with bookstores, ice-cream parlours and pastry shops. For a more local scene, head to Rua Dom Pedro V and Príncipe Real, where you'll find the creations of up-and-coming Portuguese designers and antique, *azulejo* and interior-design shops. Late-night shoppers hit Bairro Alto, where hole-in-the-wall boutiques and concept stores sell everything from vintage garb, glitzy club wear and limited-edition Adidas to cork art, ceramics and vinyl. Rua do Diário de Notícias, Rua das Salgadeiras and Rua do Norte are also worth a look.

belle-époque-style packaging for the luxury soaps, lotions and note-books are all original – resurrected from the brand's design archives. (www.clausporto.com)

Apaixonarte
DESIGN

41 MAP P42, A5

This corner design store sells only Portuguese-made home decor pieces and fashion accessories. Once a month the shop also welcomes art exhibits by local artists. Soaps, prints and small decoration items make popular souvenirs. (www.apaixonarte.com)

Cork & Company
GIFTS & SOUVENIRS

42 MAP P42, D4

At this elegantly designed shop, you'll find cork put to surprisingly imaginative uses, with well-made and sustainable cork handbags, pens, wallets, journals, hats, scarves, place mats, umbrellas, iPhone covers and even chaise longues! (www.corkandcompany.pt)

Fábrica Sant'Ana
ARTS & CRAFTS

43 MAP P42, D6

Hand-making and painting *azulejos* (from €5) since 1741, this is the place to get some eye-catching porcelain tiles for your home. (www.santanna.com.pt)

El Dorado
CLOTHING

44 MAP P42, D4

A gramophone plays vinyl classics as divas grab vintage styles, from psychedelic prints to six-inch platforms and pencil skirts, at this Bairro Alto hipster place. There's also a great range of club wear.

Livraria Bertrand
BOOKS

45 MAP P42, F5

The world's oldest operating book-shop, open since 1732 according to *Guinness World Records,* Bertrand has excellent selections, including titles in English, French and Spanish. (www.bertrand.pt)

Walking Tour 🥾

Strolling Príncipe Real

Príncipe Real, located between Bairro Alto and Rato, is an open-minded, bohemian neighbourhood, with markets, antique stores, boutiques and people-watching squares. This enclave is home to artists, up-and-coming designers and the gay community, giving it a creative, blissfully relaxed vibe.

Walk Facts

Start Esplanada Café; bus 202 or 758

End Cerveteca Lisboa; bus 202 or 758

Length 1.3km; 2 hours

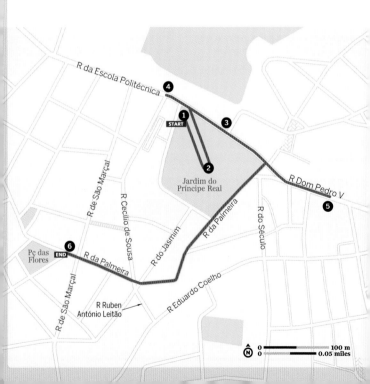

❶ Morning Coffee

Start your day in leisurely fashion at the **Esplanada Café** (www.face book.com/esplanadadoprincipereal), a tree-shaded pit stop with tables under massive rubber tree palms.

❷ Plaza Stroll

A century-old cedar tree forms a giant natural parasol at the centre of palm-dotted **Jardim do Príncipe Real**, where *lisboêtas* from all walks of life hang out. The square is rimmed by elegant 19th-century town houses; most striking of all is the powder-puff-pink **Palacete Ribeiro da Cunha** at No 26.

❸ Innovative Design

If you want to find Lisbon's cutting edge, Praça do Príncipe Real is where it's at. Designers and creatives from the emerging to the established show their latest works at gorgeous concept stores like neo-Moorish **Embaixada** (www. embaixadalx.pt).

❹ Chocolate Wonderland

Make a re-fuelling stop at one of Lisbon's most cherished *chocolatarias,* **Bettina & Niccolò Corallo** (www.claudiocorallo.com), a family-run transplant from São Tomé and Príncipe that does both exquisite chocolate and immensely satisfying coffee sourced from their family plantations in Africa.

❺ Fashion Focus

Lisbon is no longer the wallflower of the international fashion scene. The city has carved out a reputation as a catwalk capital to watch, and nowhere is this reflected more than on hip strip Rua Dom Pedro V. Check out Lidija Kolovrat's boldly patterned wonders at **Kolovrat** (www.lidijakolovrat.com), or the sustainable stylish Portuguese-made garments at **ISTO** (www.isto.pt).

❻ Craft-Beer Hideaway

For Lisbon's cosiest craft beer bar, head down to the pretty and picturesque Praça das Flores, where **Cerveteca Lisboa** (www. cervetecalisboa.com) specialises in local suds along with choice international brews, painstakingly drink-tested by friendly owners Rui and Carolina. Sipping on a cold one in this pretty plaza – though not at the kiosk tables! – is a darn satisfying end-of-day exercise.

Explore ⊚
Baixa & Rossio

Built high and mighty on the rubble of the 1755 earth-quake, Baixa is Lisbon's riverfront gateway, its royal flag-bearer, its lifeblood. Trams rumble, buskers hold crowds captive and shoppers mill around old-world stores. The main drag, Rua Augusta, links the regal Praça do Comércio to Rossio, where you'll find a neigh-bourly vibe in closet-sized ginjinha (cherry liqueur) bars and street cafes.

The Short List

○ **Igreja de São Domingos (p65)** *Pondering hundreds of years of turmoil and destruction inside this 1241 sanctuary, Lisbon's most cinematic church.*

○ **Ginjinha Bars (p70)** *Getting liquored up with the locals at sunset on shots of sour-cherry love around Largo de São Domingos.*

○ **Arco da Rua Augusta (p59)** *Taking in a bird's-eye view of the city's heart and soul, Praça do Comércio, from atop this triumphal arch.*

○ **Ribeira das Naus (p65)** *Relaxing away an afternoon with coffee or cocktails along Lisbon's revamped riverfront promenade.*

Getting There & Around

Ⓜ Baixa-Chiado, Rossio, Terreiro do Paço, Restauradores stations.

🚋 Trams 12E (circular route) and 15E to Algés via Alcântara and Belém depart from Praça da Figueira. Trams 18E and 25E stop at Praça do Comércio; tram 18 en route to Ajuda via Alcântara; and tram 25 to Campo de Ourique via Estrela. Pick up tram 28E at Rua da Conceição or Martim Moniz.

Baixa & Rossio Map on p64

Arco da Rua Augusta (p59) RONALD SUMNERS/SHUTTERSTOCK ©

Top Experience 📷
Admire Praça do Comércio

*There's no place like Praça do Comércio for the
'wow, I'm in Lisbon!' effect. Boat arrivals used
to disembark here, and it still feels like the city's
gateway, thronging with activity. With its 18th-
century arcades and triumphal arch, this is Lisbon
at its monumental best. Wander the riverfront,
gaze up at the equestrian statue, and witness the
history of Lisbon mapped out in stone.*

◎ MAP P64, C6

MARCO CRUPI/SHUTTERSTOCK ©

Arco da Rua Augusta

Built in the wake of the 1755 earthquake, this **triumphal arch** is a riot of columns crowned with allegorical figures representing Glory, Valour and Genius, and carried high by bigwigs including Vasco da Gama and Marquês de Pombal. A lift whisks you to the top, where fine views of Praça do Comércio, the river and the castle await.

Dom José I Statue

The square's centrepiece, an 18th-century equestrian statue of the king Dom José I, hints at the square's royal roots as the pre-earthquake site of Palácio da Ribeira.

Riverfront

Praça do Comércio leads elegantly down to the banks of the Rio Tejo. The riverfront promenade is a popular gathering spot, with its sweeping views, boat trips and buskers. Across the water you can glimpse the 110m-high Cristo Rei (p66).

ViniPortugal

Under the arcades, vaulted tasting room **ViniPortugal** (www.winesofportugal.info) is a viticultural organisation offering several wine tastings a day. A €3 Enocard allows you to taste at least three Portuguese wines, from Alentejo whites to full-bodied Douro reds.

Pátio da Galé

Lisbon's showpiece, the Pátio da Galé, harbours the restored inner courtyard of the former royal palace. Following a huge makeover, the complex is home to the tourist office, Lisbon Shop (p71), and people-watching cafes and restaurants.

★ Top Tips

o Come in the early morning to appreciate the square at its most peaceful, and in the evening to see its monuments beautifully lit up.

o Tie in your visit with a tour – Praça do Comércio is the starting point for many boat excursions and city walks.

✕ Take a Break

Head to nearby **Fragoleto** (www.facebook.com/geladosfragoleto) for rich, creamy Italian-style gelato, often in unusual flavours from ecologically sourced ingredients.

Quick and simple **Nova Pombalina** (www.facebook.com/anovapombalina) slings delicious *leitão* (suckling pig) sandwiches to your plate (or to go) in 60 seconds or less.

Baixa & Rossio Admire Praça do Comércio

Top Experience 📷

Unearth History at the Núcleo Arqueológico da Rua dos Correeiros

Halting construction work in Lisbon because of archaeological finds is common. Less frequent, though, is the unveiling of layers of history that go back 2,500 years. This happened in the early 1990s when workers began to lay the foundations for a parking garage. Since then, visitors have been guided through the guts of the building, discovering secrets of past civilisations.

◎ MAP P64, C5

www.fundacaomillennium
bcp.pt/nucleo-arqueo
logico

Archaeological Remains

At the beginning of the tour, the guide provides historical context through interactive maps and blueprints in a room with a glass floor that gives visitors a glimpse of three building foundations from different periods. Highlights of this section of the tour include the different artefacts on display that give out the first clues as to why Lisbon attracted so many settlers: the fertile riverbed and the abundance of fish. Sardines were the essential raw material for the high-priced *garum* (a fish-based sauce) that Romans exported.

Historical Marks

The second part of the tour, going underground via a narrow staircase, takes travellers further into the bowels of the building. The different levels of foundations built on foundations trace the various historical periods of Lisbon: the Phoenician settlements, the Islamic communities, the Roman Empire and the post-1755 earthquake reconstructed city. Traces of Iron Age hearths, large *garum*-producing tanks, part of an 18th-century sewage system, and even a medieval skeleton share the same labyrinthine space.

Ancient Urban Dwellings

Before heading out through the temporary exhibitions room, there's still time to see the remains of what was most likely a large (and wealthy) Roman house, built by the side of a road that no longer exists. From the mezzanine, visitors can see the deep stone vats for warm and cold baths, and part of an almost-intact mosaic floor.

★ Top Tip

o Scan Lisboa Romana's QR code on the pavement near the entrance to learn more about the city's Roman past.

o Ancient Roman Galleries hide underneath nearby Rua da Conceição. Twice a year (April and September) this site, run by Lisbon City Council, is open to visitors.

✕ Take a Break

o Head to **Nicolau Lisboa** (www.ilove nicolau.com) for all-day breakfast in a retro, aqua-green stylish setting.

o At sunset, raise a glass to the Rio Tejo at **Quiosque Ribeira das Naus** (www.facebook.com/Ribeira dasNausLisboa).

Baixa & Rossio Núcleo Arqueológico da Rua dos Correeiros

Walking Tour 🥾

Baixa Back in Time

In the cobbled laneways of Baixa and Rossio, bee-yellow funiculars and trams rumble up steep inclines as they have since the late 19th century, shoeshiners ply their trade and speciality stores thrive. As you stroll, you will come across thimble-sized haberdasheries, old-world patisseries and cupboard-sized ginjinha bars that serve nostalgia in a shot glass.

Walk Facts

Start Praça dos Restauradores; Ⓜ Restauradores
End A Ginjinha; Ⓜ Rossio
Length 2.2km; 2 hours

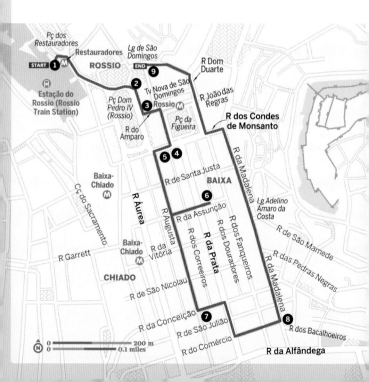

❶ Set in Stone

Easy on the eye, hard on the foot, Lisbon's mosaic cobblestones have been polished smooth over centuries. Look out for the **Calceteiro** on Praça dos Restauradores: a bronze statue of a paver, hammer in hand, which pays tribute to those who laid the city's cobblestones.

❷ Mad Hatters

Lisbon's maddest hatters, **Azevedo Rua** (www.azevedorua.pt) have been covering heads since 1886. Expect good old-fashioned service and wood-panelled cabinets full of tweedy flat caps, straw hats, bowlers and Ascot-worthy headwear.

❸ Old-School Grocer

Relive days spent shopping with grandma on and around Praça da Figueira. Close by, century-old **Manteigaria Silva** (p71) does a brisk trade in Portuguese ham, cheese, wine and *bacalhau* (dried salt-cod).

❹ Coffee & Cake

Since 1829 the patisserie **Confeitaria Nacional** (www.confeitaria nacional.com) has been expanding waistlines with its egg and almond sweets, macaroons and *pastéis de nata* (custard tarts).

❺ Portuguese Delicacies

As you make your way back towards Rossio, stop off at **Manuel Tavares** (www.manueltavares.com), a beautiful wood-fronted shop that has been tempting locals since 1860 with *pata negra* (cured ham), pungent cheeses, *ginjinha* and other treats.

❻ Vintage Valhalla

Vintage divas make for retro boutique **Outra Face da Lua** (www.facebook.com/aoutrafacedalua), crammed with puffball dresses, Lurex skirts and wildly patterned '70s shirts.

❼ Buttons & Threads

With its cluster of dark-wood-panelled, closet-sized haberdasheries, **Rua da Conceição** recalls an era where folk still used to darn stockings. Buttons, ribbons, threads and trimmings line the walls in art-nouveau **Retrosaria Bijou** and many others like it.

❽ Retro Tinned Fish

How apt that in Rua dos Bacalhoeiros ('cod-vessel street') lies 1930s shop **Conserveira de Lisboa** (www.conserveiradelisboa.pt), dedicated wholly to tinned fish, whose walls are a mosaic of retro wrappings. An elderly lady and her son tot up on a monstrous old till and wrap purchases in brown paper.

❾ Sundown Shots

Hipsters, old men in flat caps, office workers and tourists all meet at **A Ginjinha** (p70) for shots of cherry liqueur. Watch the owner line 'em up at the bar under the beady eye of the drink's 19th-century inventor, Espinheira.

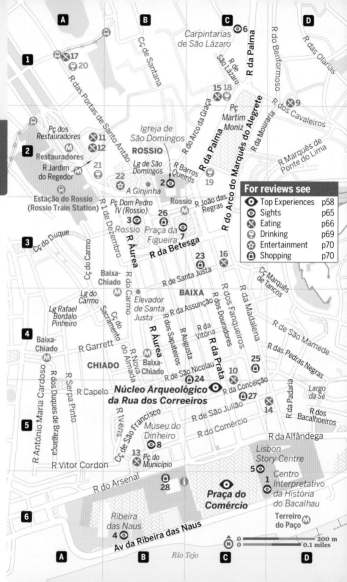

Baixa & Rossio

Carpintarias de São Lázaro

Igreja de São Domingos

ROSSIO

Pç dos Restauradores

Restauradores

R Jardim do Regedor

Estação do Rossío (Rossio Train Station)

Lg de São Domingos

A Ginjinha

Pç Dom Pedro IV (Rossio)

Rossio

Praça da Figueira

Pç Martim Moniz

Lg do Carmo

Lg Rafael Bordalo Pinheiro

Baixa-Chiado

Baixa-Chiado

Elevador de Santa Justa

CHIADO

Baixa-Chiado

BAIXA

Núcleo Arqueológico da Rua dos Correeiros

Museu do Dinheiro

Pç do Município

R do Arsenal

Ribeira das Naus

Av da Ribeira das Naus

Praça do Comércio

Lisbon Story Centre

Centro Interpretativo da História do Bacalhau

Terreiro do Paço

Largo da Sé

For reviews see	
⊙ Top Experiences	p58
⊙ Sights	p65
⊗ Eating	p66
⬤ Drinking	p69
✪ Entertainment	p70
🔒 Shopping	p70

Rio Tejo

0   200 m
0   0.1 miles

Sights

Centro Interpretativo da História do Bacalhau   MUSEUM

1 ◉ MAP P64, D6

Portugal's obsession with *bacalhau* (salted cod) isn't a mystery, but this interactive museum in Lisbon's downtown exists to answer all the questions. It establishes the economic roots of *bacalhau* fishing and even addresses the role of this 'typical' dish in the dictatorship's propaganda. Visitors, one at a time, can also safely experience the loneliness of being in a tiny boat in the middle of the vast ocean. (www.historiabacalhau.pt)

Igreja de São Domingos   CHURCH

2 ◉ MAP P64, B2

It's a miracle that this baroque church dating to 1241 still stands, having barely survived the 1755 earthquake, then fire in 1959. Its sea of tealights illuminates gashed pillars, battered walls and ethereal sculptures in its musty yet enchanting interior. Note the Star of David memorial outside, marking the spot of a bloody anti-Semitic massacre in 1506. (www.patriarcado-lisboa.pt)

Rossio   PLAZA

3 ◉ MAP P64, B3

Simply known as Rossio to locals, Praça Dom Pedro IV has 24-hour buzz. Shoeshiners, lottery-ticket sellers, hash-peddlers and office workers drift across its wave-like cobbles, gazing up to its ornate fountains and **Dom Pedro IV** (Brazil's first emperor), perched high on a marble pedestal.

Ribeira das Naus   WATERFRONT

4 ◉ MAP P64, B6

This riverfront promenade between Praça do Comércio and Cais do Sodré is a focal point along Lisbon's continually regenerating waterfront. With broad views over the Rio Tejo, it's a fine place for strolling, lounging, reading, cycling or kicking back with a coffee at the kiosk. This is the closest Lisbon gets to an urban beach.

Lisbon Story Centre   MUSEUM

5 ◉ MAP P64, C5

This museum takes visitors on a 60-minute journey through Lisbon's history, from its early foundation (pre-ancient Roman days) to modern times. An audio guide and multimedia exhibits describe key episodes, including New World colonisation, the terrifying 1755 earthquake (with a vivid film re-enacting the horrors) and the ambitious reconstruction that followed. (www.lisboastorycentre.pt)

Carpintarias de São Lázaro   CULTURAL CENTRE

6 ◉ MAP P64, C1

This cultural centre in the heart of Mouraria (a three-floor former carpenter's haunt survived a fire and years of neglect) welcomes visitors with a full calendar

Cristo Rei

Visible from almost anywhere in Lisbon, the 110m **Cristo Rei** (www.cristorei.pt) is a statue of Christ with outstretched arms. The slightly more baroque version of Rio de Janeiro's Christ the Redeemer was erected in 1959 to thank God for sparing Portugal from the horrors of WWII. A lift zooms you up to a platform, from where Lisbon spreads magnificently before you.

of temporary exhibitions, art showcases, and music and dance performances, some of them taking place at the in-house rooftop bar Miradouro de Baixo. (www.carpintariasdesaolazaro.pt)

Praça da Figueira   PLAZA

7 ◎ MAP P64, B3

Praça da Figueira is framed by whizzing traffic, Pombaline town houses and alfresco cafes with stellar views of hilltop Castelo de São Jorge. At its centre rises gallant **Dom João I**, once celebrated for his 15th-century expeditions in Africa, now targeted by pigeons and gravity-defying skateboarders.

Museu do Dinheiro   MUSEUM

8 ◎ MAP P64, B5

Pop into Banco do Portugal's money museum to see the stunning €34-million interior renovation of the once-mighty São Julião church (closed in 1933); and the more notable **Interpretation Centre for King Dinis' Wall**, a preserved 30m expanse of the 13th-century medieval city wall, located in the church's former crypt and discov-

ered during a 2010 excavation. (www.museudodinheiro.pt)

Eating

Mi Dai   CHINESE €

9 ✕ MAP P64, D1

Probably one of *lisboêtas'* best-kept secrets when it comes to affordable restaurants in Martim Moniz. This blink-and-you-might-miss-it, cash-only, canteen-style spot is one of the most authentic places for Chinese food in Lisbon. Without a fixed menu, customers pick out the ingredients they want wok-fried, with a side of white rice. Undecided? Go for the aubergine. (Cantina Chinesa)

Pizzeria Romana al Taglio   PIZZA €

10 ✕ MAP P64, C4

This Roman transplant dishes out fresh and fast *pizza al taglio* (traditional, Roman-style pizza in square slices) in some 25 ridiculously inviting flavours, including at least a dozen vegan/veg options. Popular choices such as *Cuor di Latte* (buffalo mozzarella, tomato, basil) and *Boscaiola* (mushrooms and sausage) make for a great on-the-go meal while pounding Baixa's cobblestones. (www.romanapizza.it)

Bonjardim

PORTUGUESE €€

11 MAP P64, A2

Juicy, spit-roast *frango* (chicken) is served with a mountain of fries at this no-frills joint. Add piri-piri (hot sauce) for extra spice. The pavement terrace is elbow-to-elbow in summer.

Pinóquio

PORTUGUESE €€

12 MAP P64, A2

Busy Pinóquio is easy to miss as it's tucked into a *praça* corner partially obstructed by a souvenir kiosk. Dressed in white tablecloths against pea-green walls, it's distinctly old school, with indomitable waiters slinging a stunning slew of classic dishes: *arroz de pato* (duck rice), seafood *feijoada*, *arroz de bacalhau* (codfish rice), and pork chops with almonds and coriander. (www.restaurantepinoquio.pt)

Delfina – Cantina Portuguesa

PORTUGUESE €€

13 MAP P64, B5

The restaurant at boutique hotel Alma Lusa embodies the spirit of typical Portuguese cuisine. The menu mixes staple dishes like *bacalhau à Brás* (shredded cod with onions, eggs and potatoes) with reinventions of traditional recipes that you'll find in the Delfina's Choices section, including an extensive and unconventional *açorda* (bread and shellfish stew) menu. (www.almalusahotels.com/delfina)

Tasca Kome

JAPANESE €€

14 MAP P64, D5

This blink-and-you'll-miss-it Japanese *tasca* is one of Lisbon's few turning out authentic cuisine from the Land of the Rising Sun. The menu doesn't overwhelm with options; instead, there's exquisite sushi, *tonkatsu* (breaded pork cutlets), *aji tataki* (horse mackerel with ginger and chives), *nasu dengaku* (fried aubergine with

Baixa & Rossio Eating

Grand Views

If the lanky, wrought-iron **Elevador de Santa Justa** (Map p64, B4; www.carris.pt/en) seems uncannily familiar, it's probably because the neo-Gothic marvel is the handiwork of Raul Mésnier, Gustave Eiffel's apprentice. It's Lisbon's only vertical street lift, built in 1902 and steam-powered until 1907. Get here early to beat the crowds and zoom to the top for sweeping views over the city's skyline.

Bear in mind, however, that some call the €5.15 fee Santa *Injusta*! You can save €3.50 by entering the platform from the top (behind Convento do Carmo via Bellalisa restaurant).

The Earthquake that Shook Lisbon

The Fall of a Thriving City

Picture, if you can, Lisbon in its heyday: Portugal has unearthed gold in Brazil; merchants are flocking to the city to trade in gold, spices, silks and jewels; the city is a magnificent canvas of 16th-century Manueline architecture. At the heart of it all is Baixa and the royal Palácio da Ribeira rising triumphantly above Terreiro do Paço square.

Now fast-forward to 9.40am on All Saints' Day, 1 November 1755: the day that everything changed. Three major earthquakes hit as residents celebrated Mass. The tremors brought an even more devastating fire and tsunami. Much of the city fell like a pack of dominoes, never to regain its former status; palaces, libraries, art galleries, churches and hospitals were razed to the ground. Some estimate that as many as 90,000 of Lisbon's 270,000 inhabitants died.

The Rise of Baixa & Pombaline Architecture

Enter the formidable, unflappable, geometrically minded Sebastião de Melo, better known as the Marquês de Pombal. As Dom João I's chief minister, the Marquês de Pombal swiftly set about reconstructing the city, good to his word to 'bury the dead and heal the living'. In the wake of the disaster, the autocratic statesman not only kept the country's head above water as it was plunged into economic chaos, but he also managed to propel Lisbon into the modern era.

Together with military engineers and architects Eugenio dos Santos and Manuel da Maia, the Marquês de Pombal played a pivotal role in reconstructing the city in a simple, cheap, earthquake-proof way that created today's formal grid, and Pombaline style was born. The antithesis of rococo, Pombaline architecture was functional and restrained: *azulejos* (hand-painted tiles) and decorative elements were used sparingly, building materials were prefabricated, and wide streets and broad plazas were preferred.

The best example of Pombaline style is the Baixa Pombalina, delineated by Rossio to the north and Praça do Comércio to the south. The neighbourhood has been on the Unesco list of tentative World Heritage Sites since 2004.

miso) and daily-changing specials that bridge cultures (pork stew with daikon, for example). (www.kome-lisboa.com)

Kin

ASIAN €€

15 🍽 MAP P64, C1

Topo's sexy Asian lounge – adjacent to its original rooftop location inside a Praça Martim Moniz commercial centre – is a Thai/Vietnamese/Indonesian/Chinese foursome under the watchful eye of a Chinese dragon figure draped overhead. Mostly Asian noodle and rice dishes (*pad thai, nasi goreng*) are paired with craft cocktails designed to complement the sweet and spice of the dishes. (www.topo-lisboa.pt)

Terraço Editorial   PORTUGUESE €€

16  MAP P64, C3

This spot on the once underappreciated top floor of the kitchenware store Pollux with a view of Lisbon's landmarks, including iconic Elevador de Santa Justa and the Carmo Convent ruins, has had many incarnations. Now it's a bar/restaurant with *petiscos* on the menu and a long list of wines to experience by the glass or by the bottle. (www.terracoeditorial.pt)

Solar dos Presuntos   PORTUGUESE €€€

17 MAP P64, A1

Don't be fooled by the smoked *presunto* (ham) hanging in the window, this iconic restaurant is renowned for its excellent seafood too. Start with the excellent *pata negra* (cured ham), *paio* smoked sausage and cheese *couvert* (stew), then dig into a fantastic lobster *açorda,* delectable seafood paella or crustacean curry. (www.solardospresuntos.com)

Drinking

TOPO Martim Moniz   COCKTAIL BAR

18 MAP P64, C1

This hipster hangout is an excellent rooftop lounge with extraordinary views over lively Praça Martim Moniz and the whole of Lisbon. It features open-air wooden benches for cocktails (€8 to €14), coffee and light bites, and a covered indoor lounge. It's set to a vibey soundtrack, often courtesy of DJs. (www.facebook.com/pg/topolisboa)

Rooftop Bar   BAR

19 MAP P64, C2

Grab a table at sundown on the Hotel Mundial's roof terrace for a

Elevador de Santa Justa (p67)

TRABANTOS/SHUTTERSTOCK ©

sweeping view of Lisbon and its hilltop castle. The backlit bar, white sofas and ambient sounds set the stage for evening drinks and sharing plates. (www.hotel-mundial.pt)

Fábrica Coffee Roasters

COFFEE

20 🚌 MAP P64, A1

Keep on walking past the touristy restaurants along pedestrianised Rua das Portas de Santo Antão to this sublime coffee temple, where serious caffeine is served amid a hodgepodge of exposed brick, hardwood floors and mismatched vintage furniture. Single-origin arabica beans from Brazil, Ethiopia and Colombia are roasted in-house and churned into distinctly third-wave cups of joe. Connoisseurs rejoice! (www.fabricacoffee roasters.com)

Rossio Gastrobar

BAR

21 🚌 MAP P64, A2

A terrific rooftop spot for an afternoon coffee or drinks (cocktails from €9 to €17) as the city lights begin to glow. From 12.30pm to midnight nibble through a menu of Portuguese *petiscos* (the oxtail croquettes with homemade mustard are highly recommended) and Japanese-inspired light dishes made with seasonal ingredients. (www.altishotels.com)

Entertainment

Teatro Nacional de Dona Maria II

THEATRE

22 ⭐ MAP P64, B2

Rossio's graceful neoclassical theatre has a somewhat hit-and-miss schedule. Guided tours on Mondays (except August) are at 11am (€8). (www.teatro-dmaria.pt)

Shopping

Garrafeira Nacional

WINE

23 🔒 MAP P64, C3

This Lisbon landmark has been selling Portuguese wine since 1927 and is easily the best spot to pick up a bevy of local wines and spirits. It is especially helpful and will steer you towards lesser-known boutique wines and vintage ports in addition to the usual suspects. The small museum features vintages dating to the 18th century. (www.garrafeiranacional.com)

Typographia

CLOTHING

24 MAP P64, C4

With stores in Porto and Madrid as well, this high-design T-shirt shop is one of Europe's best. It features a select, monthly changing array of clever and artsy, locally designed T-shirts (€23.95), which no one else will be wearing back home. (www.typographia.com)

Soma Ideas

ARTS & CRAFTS

25 MAP P64, C4

Traditional Portuguese imagery gets a modern, design-forward twist at this not-so-average souvenir shop. Colourful coffee mugs, ceramics and framed art dominate – you won't regret your purchases a year later! (www.somaideas.com)

Manteigaria Silva

FOOD

26 MAP P64, B3

Specialising in the best of the best and in business for more than a century, Manteigaria Silva does a brisk trade in staunchly curated Portuguese ham, cheese, wine and *bacalhau*. (www.manteigariasilva.pt)

Espaço Açores

FOOD

27 MAP P64, C5

The closest you can get to actually visiting the Azores in Lisbon is this

Portuguese Inquisition

The neoclassical grandeur of **Teatro Nacional de Dona Maria II** evokes nothing of its sinister background as Palácio dos Estaus, seat of the Portuguese Inquisition from 1540. Those found guilty of heresy, witchcraft or practising Judaism were publicly executed on Praça Dom Pedro IV (Rossio) or Largo de São Domingos. Though Dom João III – *o Piedoso* (the Pious) – launched the Inquisition in 1536, the persecution of Jews goes back further; look for the Star of David in front of Igreja de São Domingos, which marks the spot of a bloody anti-Semitic massacre in 1506.

attractive shop, where a taste of the islands comes in the form of cheese, honey, preserves, passion-fruit liqueur and, apparently, the oldest tea produced in Europe.

Lisbon Shop

GIFTS & SOUVENIRS

28 MAP P64, B6

Housed in the Pombaline Pátio da Galé complex, this shop is crammed with Portuguese gifts, from tram T-shirts, cockerel mugs and cork bags to speciality foods. It's run by Ask Me Lisboa, the public face of Lisbon tourism. (www.askmelisboa.com)

Walking Tour 🥾

Baixa to Santa Catarina

Shopping in Baixa's old-world stores, culture in Chiado's museums, captivating sunset views from Santa Catarina – it's all packed into this 'greatest hits' tour of downtown Lisbon. This afternoon walk gives you a palpable sense of Lisbon's history – on Baixa's regal plazas, in Pombaline backstreets built in the wake of the 1755 earthquake, and in literary-flavoured cafes, where poets like Fernando Pessoa once hung out.

Walk Facts

Start Praça do Comércio; Ⓜ Terreiro do Paço

Finish Santa Catarina; 🚋 28

Length 4.5km; 3½ hours

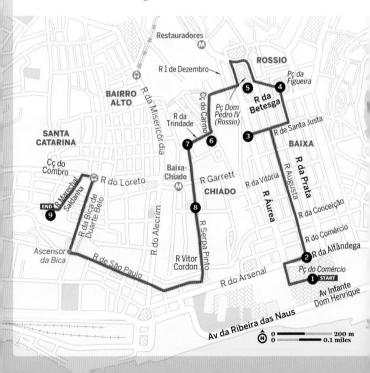

❶ Praça do Comércio

At Lisbon's riverside gateway, **Praça do Comércio** (p58), trams rumble past palatial facades, arcades and a gallant equestrian statue of Dom José I. Nip into **ViniPortugal** (p59) to taste Portuguese wines for €3.

❷ Rua Augusta

Pass through the triumphal **Arco da Rua Augusta** (p59) onto the main thoroughfare, Rua Augusta, buzzing with street entertainers and shoppers. From here, explore backstreets like old-fashioned **Rua da Conceição**.

❸ Elevador de Santa Justa

When you hit Rua de Santa Justa, swing left for the neo-Gothic **Elevador de Santa Justa** (p67), Lisbon's only vertical street lift. Enjoy the view from outside the lift or walk 100m to **Terraços do Carmo**.

❹ Praça da Figueira

Saunter east along Rua de Santa Justa then north up Rua da Prata to **Praça da Figueira** (p66) for castle views from below. The square is rimmed with cafes and old-school stores.

❺ Rossio

Head straight onto **Rossio** (p65), one of Lisbon's grandest squares with its wave-like cobbles, fountains, neoclassical theatre and neo-Manueline Estação do Rossio.

❻ Largo do Carmo

Behind the train station, Calçada do Carmo climbs to Chiado's Largo do Carmo, where jacaranda trees shade pavement cafes and the 18th-century Chafariz do Carmo fountain. Rising above it are the ethereal arches of the ruined **Convento do Carmo** (p38).

❼ Casa do Ferreira das Tabuletas

Cross the square to Rua da Trindade and the 1864 **Casa do Ferreira das Tabuletas**, where the trompe l'œil *azulejos* (hand-painted tiles) depict allegorical figures and the elements.

❽ Rua Serpa Pinto

Follow the road south, past the 18th-century opera house **Teatro Nacional de São Carlos** (p51). Further on is modern-art gallery **Museu do Chiado** (p44).

❾ Santa Catarina

Turn right and follow the trams along elegant Rua de São Paulo for a ride on the 1892 **Elevador da Bica** (p44). Descend Rua Marechal Saldanha to **Miradouro de Santa Catarina** (p44) for sunset views of the river.

Top Experience 📸
Take a Scenic Ride on Tram 28

There's a reason why tram 28E tops most travellers' Lisbon wishlists. This rickety, screechy, gloriously old-fashioned ride from Praça Martim Moniz to Campo de Ourique provides 45 minutes of mood-lifting views and absurdly steep climbs. Or, for a less touristy experience, seek out some of the other routes that traverse Lisbon's hills. Either way, prepare for a city tour to remember.

The Route

Starting in Praça Martim Moniz, tram 28E scoots along the narrow, curving backstreets of Graça before descending past the **Sé** (cathedral). Jump off at **Largo das Portas do Sol** for an incredible city panorama, or make the short climb up to **Castelo de São Jorge**.

Settle back as you rumble through the Pombaline streets of Baixa to the mosaic-tiled **Praça Luís de Camões**, centred on a statue of its eponymous poet.

As the tram continues past *azulejo*-tiled, pastel-hued facades on the Calçada da Estrela, the neoclassical **Assembleia da República** and the graceful white dome of the baroque **Basílica da Estrela** slide into view.

Stay right until the end (Campo de Ourique) for a stroll around 1833's **Cemitério dos Prazeres**, dotted with tombs and commanding views of the river and Ponte 25 de Abril.

Reducing Impact

Contrary to popular belief, tram 28E isn't a tourist ride but much-needed public transportation for *lisboêtas* living in the historic centre. Reduce your impact on their commutes by avoiding rush hour (7am to 9am and 5pm to 7pm) or opting for the paid Hills Tramcar Tour (from €22; red trams depart from **Praça do Comércio**).

Other Classic Tram Routes

Get the authentic tram experience without the crowds by seeking out lesser-known routes. **Tram 12** (pictured) travels from Martim Moniz and back, via *miradouros* Portas do Sol and Santa Luzia, and Sé. **Tram 25** connects café-lined Praça da Figueira to Campo de Ourique via nightlife hotspots Cais do Sodré and Santos. And the revived **tram 24** goes from busy Praça Luís de Camões to Campolide, across stylish Príncipe Real and offbeat Amoreiras.

★ Top Tips

○ Mind your personal belongings – tram 28E is fertile ground for pickpockets.

○ Your best bet for snagging a seat is entering the tram at the beginning or end of the route (Martim Moniz or Campo de Ourique).

○ Want to hop on and off at your leisure? Invest in a 24-hour Carris pass (€6.40), which covers all trams and funiculars.

✕ Take a Break

Hop off tram 28 at the Graça stop and hop in Damas (p91) if you're travelling here in the afternoon. Have a snack or a cocktail to the beat of whatever's playing that day.

Disembark from tram 25 one stop before the final Campo de Ourique stop, near the church, and enjoy local life and a casual lunch at **Mercado de Campo de Ourique** (www. facebook.com/ mercadodecampode ourique/).

Explore ⊗

Mouraria, Alfama & Graça

This is the Lisbon you have no doubt dreamed about: a medieval-style castle slung on a hillside, cobbled alleys twisting to sky-high viewpoints and laundry-strung houses in a fresco-painter's palette of colours. In this corner of the city, life is played out on the streets. Fado still rocks as it did way back when, one-pan family bistros fire up their grills at lunchtime, and the neighbourly vibe keeps things alluringly low-key.

The Short List

○ **Alfama** Wandering the labyrinthine lanes of this medieval and Moorish time capsule.

○ **Castelo de São Jorge (p78)** Roaming the ramparts of these mid-11th-century hilltop fortifications.

○ **Largo das Portas do Sol (p81)** Kicking back with a coffee or cocktail with the best views of the river and the rust-shaded jumble of rooftops over Alfama.

○ **Museu do Aljube (p84)** Contemplating the haunting reality of life under Europe's longest dictatorship at this museum inside a former political prison.

Getting There & Around

🚊 Tram 28E bowls through Mouraria and Graça. Key stops: Largo das Portas do Sol, Sé and Largo da Graça.

Ⓜ The blue line to Santa Apolónia is a quick way of reaching the sights closest to the river.

🚌 Take the 734 from Martim Moniz to Santa Apolónia train station for Largo da Graça and Campo de Santa Clara.

Mouraria, Alfama & Graça Map on p82

Top Experience 📷
Explore Castelo de São Jorge

Gazing grandly over the city, these heavily re-stored hilltop fortifications evoke Lisbon's history from the bold to the bloody. The castle dates to the mid-11th century when the Moors ruled Lisbon and the stronghold was the heart of their alcáçova (citadel). Christian crusaders in 1147, royals from the 14th to 16th centuries, and convicts in every century – this castle has seen it all.

◎ MAP P82, B3

www.castelodesaojorge.pt

Ramparts & Garden

Shaded by pine trees, the castle's ramparts afford far-reaching views over Lisbon. From here you can glimpse the river and Ponte 25 de Abril, contrast the grid-like streets of Baixa with the high-rises of the modern districts, and pick out the city's monuments and plazas. Peacocks strut proudly through the adjacent gardens, littered with ruins.

Tower of Ulysses & Periscope

Of all the castle's 11 towers, the Tower of Ulysses has the most gripping history. It once housed the royal treasury and archives, and was nicknamed the Torre do Tombo (Tumbling Tower) because the most important things in the kingdom used to 'tumble' into it. It now contains a periscope, or camera obscura, which gives a 360-degree view of the city in real time.

Núcleo Museológico

This museum makes a fair stab at drawing together the different epochs of the castle's history (and prehistory) and spelling them out in artefacts. On display is the fruit of archaeological digs – fragments of Iron Age pottery, Roman wine vessels, medieval oil lamps and coins, 17th-century *azulejos* (hand-painted tiles) and the like.

Archaeological Site

OK, it's time to use your imagination to piece together the parts of the castle's past with a wander around this archaeological site. In a quiet corner of the fortress, you can just about make out where the first settlement was in the 7th century BCE, the remains of the mid-11th-century Moorish dwellings and the ruins of the last royal residence, destroyed in the 1755 earthquake.

★ Top Tips

○ Join one of the free 1½-hour guided tours of the castle at 10.30am, 1pm and 4pm daily. Free 20-minute tours of the Tower of Ulysses run every 20 minutes.

○ Pick up a free map and guide at the entrance.

○ Arrive early or late in the day for fewer crowds.

○ Come back at dusk for perfect snapshots of the illuminated castle.

✕ Take a Break

By day, follow the scent of chargrilled fish to local favourite **Páteo 13** (www.facebook.com/pateo13), tucked away on a small, festively decorated plaza in Alfama.

By night, enjoy Portuguese food with a side of live fado music at Graça's **Tasca do Jaime**.

Walking Tour 🥾

Alfama Backstreets

Alfama and its neighbours, Graça and Mouraria, afford snapshots of daily life on flower-draped squares, at weekend flea markets, and in hidden alleys full of unexpected beauty and banter.

Walk Facts

Start Miradouro de Santa Luzia; 🚋28E

End Miradouro da Senhora do Monte; 🚋28E

Length 5km; two to three hours

❶ River Gazing

Views across Alfama's rooftops to the Rio Tejo beckon from the bougainvillea-wreathed **Miradouro de Santa Luzia** on Rua do Limoeiro. At the back, note the blue-and-white *azulejo* tile panels depicting scenes from the Siege of Lisbon in 1147 and the early-18th-century Praça do Comércio.

❷ Castelo's Side Streets

Few explore the atmospheric web of lanes around Castelo de São Jorge, such as **Rua Santa Cruz do Castelo**, studded with pastel-hued houses, hole-in-the-wall bars and grocers. Slow the pace here for a sense of the old Moorish *alcáçova* (citadel), once home to the city's elite.

❸ Moorish Gateway

The Moorish gateway **Largo das Portas do Sol** has postcard views of Alfama and Graça. Peer across a mosaic of red rooftops to the Panteão Nacional's ivory-white dome and twin-spired Igreja de São Vicente de Fora.

❹ Hidden Azulejos

Following the tram tracks downhill brings you to Sé, Lisbon's imposing Gothic cathedral. Behind it is **Rua de São João da Praça**, with vaulted cafes, fado clubs and *azulejo*-clad facades – look for diamond-tip patterns at No 88 and floral motifs at No 106.

❺ Alfama Stroll

At Alfama's higgledy-piggledy heart is **Largo de São Miguel**, identified by its twin-towered chapel and palm tree, and **Rua dos Remédios**, with its cafes, grocery stores and galleries. Close by, melancholic fado drifts from open windows, men play backgammon and neighbours trade gossip just as they have for centuries.

❻ Flea-Market Finds

To see Graça at its lively best, visit on Tuesday or Saturday when **Campo de Santa Clara** becomes the giant **Feira da Ladra** (p91) (flea market), with locals gathering to sell tat and treasures in the shadow of the gracefully domed Panteão Nacional.

❼ Summertime Hangout

A much-loved summertime hangout, **Miradouro da Graça**, near the baroque Igreja da Graça, has an incredible vista to the castle on the hillside, the river and the Ponte 25 de Abril. Sunset is prime-time viewing.

❽ Lisbon's Highest Viewpoint

For a top-of-the-city view, huff up to **Miradouro da Senhora do Monte**, one of the lesser-known *miradouros* in Lisbon, despite being the highest. From this pine-shaded plaza, the entire city spreads out picturesquely before you.

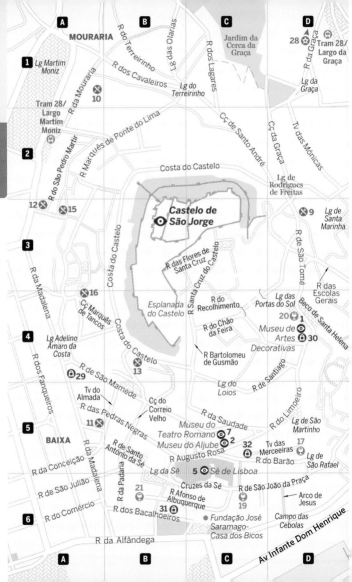

MOURARIA

R do Terreirinho

R das Olarias

Jardim da
Cerca da
Graça

R dos Lagares

A **B** **C** **D**

1 Lg Martim
Moniz

R da Mouraria

R dos Cavaleiros

Lg do
Terreirinho

28 ★

R da Graça

Tram 28/
Largo da
Graça

Lg da
Graça

10 ☒

Tram 28/
Largo
Martim
Moniz

R do São Pedro Martir

R Marquês de Ponte do Lima

Cç de Santo André

Cç da Graça

Tv das Mónicas

2

Costa do Castelo

Lg de
Rodrigues
de Freitas

12 ☒ **15** ☒

**Castelo de
São Jorge** ⊙

9 ☒

Lg de
Santa
Marinha

Costa do Castelo

R das Flores de
Santa Cruz

R de São Tomé

3

R da Madalena

R Santa Cruz do Castelo

R das
Escolas
Gerais

Beco de Santa Helena

16 ☒

Cç Marquês
de Tancos

Esplanada
do Castelo

R do
Recolhimento

Lg das
Portas do Sol

20 ☉ **1**

Museu de ⊙
Artes **30** 🏛
Decorativas

4

Lg Adelino
Amaro da
Costa

R dos Fanqueiros

Costa do Castelo

R do Chão
da Feira

R Bartolomeu
de Gusmão

R de Santiago

29 🔒

R de São Mamede

13 ☒

Lg do
Loios

Tv do
Almada

Cç do
Correio
Velho

R das Pedras Negras

R da Saudade

R de Limoeiro

Lg de São
Martinho

5

BAIXA

11 ☒

Museu do
Teatro Romano ⊙ **7**
Museu do Aljube ⊙ **2**

32 🔒

Tv das
Merceeiras

17 🏛

R do Barão

Lg de
São Rafael

R de Santo
António da Sé

R Augusto Rosa

R da Conceição

R de São Julião

R da Madalena

R da Padaria

21 🏛

Lg da Sé

Cruzes da Sé

5 ☉ **Sé de Lisboa**

R de São João da Praça

19 🏛

Arco de
Jesus

6

R do Comércio

R dos Bacalhoeiros

31 🏛

R Afonso de
Albuquerque

● Fundação José
Saramago-
Casa dos Bicos

Campo das
Cebolas

R da Alfândega

Av Infante Dom Henrique

A **B** **C** **D**

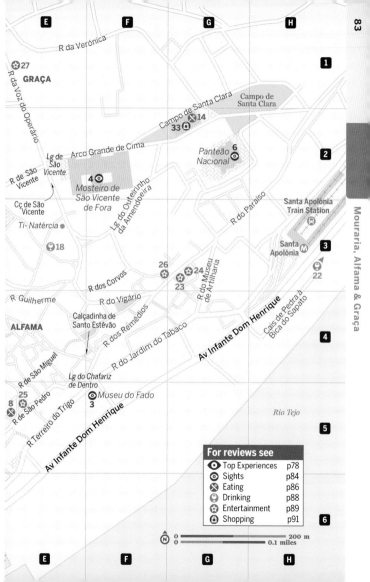

E

F

G

H

R da Verónica

GRAÇA

⊙ 27

R da Voz do Operário

1

R de São Vicente

Lg de São Vicente

Arco Grande de Cima

Campo de Santa Clara

Campo de Santa Clara

33 ⊗ 14

2

Cç de São Vicente

4 ⊙

Mosteiro de São Vicente de Fora

Panteão Nacional 6 ⊙

Lg do Outeirinho da Amendoeira

R do Paraíso

Santa Apolónia Train Station

Ti- Natércia ●

⊖ 18

R dos Corvos

26 ✪

✪ 24

23 ✪

Santa Apolónia Ⓜ

3

⊕ 22

R Guilherme

R do Vigário

R do Museu de Artilharia

ALFAMA

Calçadinha de Santo Estêvão

R dos Remédios

R do Jardim do Tabaco

Av Infante Dom Henrique

Cais de Pedra à Bica do Sapato

4

R de São Miguel

Lg do Chafariz de Dentro

25

8 ⊗

R de São Pedro

⊙ Museu do Fado

3

R Terreiro do Trigo

Rio Tejo

5

Av Infante Dom Henrique

For reviews see

⊙	Top Experiences	p78
⊙	Sights	p84
⊗	Eating	p86
⊖	Drinking	p88
✪	Entertainment	p89
⊖	Shopping	p91

N

0 ————— 200 m
0 ————— 0.1 miles

6

E

F

G

H

Mouraria, Alfama & Graça

Sights

Museu de Artes Decorativas
MUSEUM

1 MAP P82, D4

Set in a petite 17th-century palace, this museum creaks under the weight of treasures including blingy French silverware, priceless Qing vases and Indo-Chinese furniture – a collection amassed by a wealthy Portuguese banker from the age of 16. It's worth a visit just to admire the lavish apartments, embellished with baroque *azulejos,* frescos and chandeliers. (Museum of Decorative Arts; www. fress.pt)

José Saramago Foundation

Long closed to the public, the Casa dos Bicos today houses the **Fundação José Saramago** (Map p82, C6; www.josesaramago.org), with a small museum dedicated to Portugal's most famous writer, and a ground-floor excavation of Roman ruins. Opposite the Casa dos Bicos stands an olive tree, where Saramago's ashes were scattered in 2011. With its historic resonance and location close to the river, there could not be a more fitting tribute than this 16th-century landmark for the country's literary heavyweight.

Museu do Aljube
MUSEUM

2 MAP P82, C5

Both poignant and haunting, this new and highly important museum has turned the former Portuguese dictatorship's political prison of choice into a museum of truth and consequence, memorial and remembrance – it's a must-see. Disturbing tales of authoritarian dictatorship are found over three floors (beginning with the *Ditadura Militar* in 1926, and evolving into the *Estado Novo*, or New State, from 1933 to 1974), including those of government torture, eavesdropping, oppression, coercion, informing and censorship. (www.museudoaljube.pt)

Museu do Fado
MUSEUM

3 MAP P82, F5

Fado (traditional Portuguese melancholic song) was born in Alfama. Immerse yourself in its bittersweet symphonies at Museu do Fado. This engaging museum traces fado's history from its working-class roots to international stardom. (www.museudofado.pt)

Mosteiro de São Vicente de Fora
CHURCH

4 MAP P82, F2

Graça's Mosteiro de São Vicente de Fora was founded in 1147 and revamped by Italian architect Felipe Terzi in the late 16th century. Since the adjacent church took the brunt of the 1755 earthquake (the

Mosteiro de São Vicente de Fora

church's dome crashed through the ceiling of the **sacristy**, but emerged otherwise unscathed), elaborate blue-and-white *azulejos* dance across almost every wall, echoing the building's architectural curves.

Sé de Lisboa   CATHEDRAL

5 ◉ MAP P82, C5

The fortress-like Sé de Lisboa is one of Lisbon's icons, built in 1150 on the site of a mosque soon after Christians took the city from the Moors. It was sensitively restored in the 1930s. Despite the masses outside, the rib-vaulted interior, lit by a rose window, is calm. Stroll around the cathedral to spy leering gargoyles above the orange trees.

Panteão Nacional   MUSEUM

6 ◉ MAP P82, G2

Perched high and mighty above Graça's Campo de Santa Clara, the porcelain-white Panteão Nacional is a baroque beauty. Originally intended as a church, it now pays homage to Portugal's heroes and heroines, including 15th-century seafarer Vasco da Gama and *fadista* (fado singer) Amália Rodrigues. (www.panteaonacional.gov.pt)

Museu do Teatro Romano   MUSEUM

7 ◉ MAP P82, C5

The ultramodern Museu do Teatro Romano catapults you back to Emperor Augustus' rule in Olisipo (Lisbon). The star attraction is a ruined **Roman theatre**, extended in 57 CE, buried in the 1755 earthquake and finally unearthed in 1964 (you can enter for free). (Roman Theatre Museum; www.museudelisboa.pt)

Eating

Medrosa d'Alfama   CAFE €

8 🗺 MAP P82, E5

This friendly cafe has a handful of tables on one of Alfama's prettiest squares. It's a fine spot for a craft beer with grilled chorizo, *tibornos* (Portuguese-style bruschetta – try the goat's milk cheese with walnuts and honey), a €2.50 glass of sangria or a quick caffeine jolt. (www.medrosadalfama.pt)

Marcelino Pão e Vinho   PORTUGUESE €

9 🗺 MAP P82, D3

What this narrow cafe lacks in space it makes up for in atmosphere, with local artworks on the walls, occasional live music, traditional hats suspended from the ceiling and wine-crate-lined walls. It's a cosy spot for refreshing sangria, and salads, cheeseboards, sandwiches, quiches and tapas, including a fun meat grill flamed up tableside in traditional crockware.

Zé da Mouraria   PORTUGUESE €€

10 🗺 MAP P82, A1

Don't be fooled by the saloon-like doors, there's a typical Portuguese

tasca (tavern) inside: homey local cuisine, blue-and-white-tiled walls, chequered tablecloths – and it's one of Lisbon's best. The house-baked cod loaded with chickpeas, onions, garlic and olive oil is rightfully popular, and daily specials (duck rice on Wednesday!) make return trips tempting. Service is a lost cause, however.

Prado   PORTUGUESE €€

11 🗺 MAP P82, A5

This all-organic small-plates farm-to-table restaurant is the project of Chef António Galapito, after his stint at Taberna do Mercado (Michelin-star chef Nuno Mendes' Portuguese restaurant in London). Beautifully presented plates explode with fresh, clean flavours and change daily (the only dishes repeated are the cockles with spinach, coriander and fried bread, and the Barrosã beef tartare with grilled galega cabbage). (www.pradorestaurante.com)

Tasca Zé dos Cornos   PORTUGUESE €€

12 🗺 MAP P82, A3

This family-owned Mouraria tavern welcomes regulars and first-timers with the same undivided attention. Space is tight so sharing tables is the norm and so is a queue out the door. The menu contains typical Portuguese cuisine with an emphasis on pork (the ribs come highly recommended) and *bacalhau* (dried salt-cod) grilled on the spot. Portions are generous. (www.facebook.com/ZeCornos)

Chapitô à Mesa   PORTUGUESE €€

13 MAP P82, B4

At this circus school's casual cafe, the decidedly creative menu of Chef Bertílio Gomes is served alongside views worth writing home about. His modern takes include classic dishes (*bacalhau à Brás,* pork cheeks with clams, baked octopus with sweet potatoes and tomato frittata) that go swimmingly with a drop of Quinta da Silveira Reserva wine. (www.chapito.org)

Santa Clara dos Cogumelos   INTERNATIONAL €€

14 MAP P82, G2

Mushroom fans unite! This Italian-owned, Italian-executed restaurant in the old Campo de Santa Clara market hall is simply magic. The menu devotes proper patronage to the humble *cogumelo* (mushroom). The organic shiitake *à bulhão pato* (with garlic and coriander), porcini risotto with black trumpets, orange peel, rosemary and walnuts, and the porcini ice cream with glazed chestnuts are all outstanding. (www.santaclara doscogumelos.com)

Cantinho do Aziz   MOZAMBICAN €€

15 MAP P82, A3

Hidden away in a narrow alleyway in the culturally diverse quarter of Mouraria, festive Cantinho do Aziz gets top marks for excellent Mozambican cuisine. When you can't stomach any more sardine or *bacalhau,* head here for highly recommended *pulao do cabrito* (curried goat), *chacuti de cabrito* (goat in dark coconut sauce) or *makoufe* (shrimp and crab curry with peanut and coconut rice). (www.cantinhodoaziz.com)

O Velho Eurico   PORTUGUESE €€

16 MAP P82, A4

Named after the former owner, this *tasca* near Castelo de São Jorge (p78) was taken over by young chefs in 2018 who, despite the different generation, stayed true to the typical restaurant's roots. The menu includes classic dishes with *bacalhau* (salted cod) and octopus, and *petiscos* to share. (reservas.ovelhoeurico@gmail.com)

Dine with Aunty 🍽️

It's nearly impossible to find a quality restaurant in Alfama that doesn't exist for tourism purposes, but there is one. Even Portuguese President Marcelo Rebelo de Sousa has been seduced by the home-style food and crack-up character of **Ti-Natércia** (Map p82; E3; literally, 'Aunt Natércia'), a one-woman show deep in the heart of Alfama.

Drinking

Memmo Alfama
BAR

17 MAP P82, D5

Alfama unfolds like origami from the stylishly decked roof terrace of the **Memmo Alfama hotel** (www.memmoalfama.com). It's a perfect sundowner place, with dreamy vistas over the rooftops, spires and down to the Rio Tejo (and, unfortunately, the cruise ship terminal). Cocktails cost €7.50 to €10. (www.memmoalfama.com)

Copenhagen Coffee Lab
COFFEE

18 MAP P82, E3

The location of this Danish-based speciality coffee house – Lisbon's third – is the perfect pit stop while wandering the cinematic lanes of Alfama. The biggest of their three spaces feels less Nordic among the ancient Alfama stone walls, and is a more bakery-centric operation, with pastries, breakfasts (€10) and sandwiches (€6 to €8). The coffee is some of Lisbon's best. (www.copenhagencoffeelab.com)

Crafty Corner
CRAFT BEER

19 MAP P82, C6

Crafty Corner picked up its weathered leather sofas and stools and switched locations from Cais do Sodré to this address near Lisbon's Sé Cathedral. Everything else remains the same: 12 taps of Lisbon-based craft beer and casual meals, at a laid-back environment to the beat of classic rock and pop music or the occasional live concert. (www.craftycornerlisboa.com)

Portas do Sol
BAR

20 MAP P82, D4

Near one of the city's iconic viewpoints, this spacious sun-drenched terrace has a mix of sofas and white patio furniture, where you can sip cocktails (€7) while taking in magnificent river views. DJs animate to the darkly lit industrial interior on weekends. (www.portasdosol.pt)

Outro Lado
CRAFT BEER

21 MAP P82, B6

An Egyptian-Polish couple took over and seriously upgraded Lisbeer, one of Lisbon's loungiest and least beer-geeky craft-beer bars, in late 2018. Sé's Outro Lado offers 15 artisanal brews on draught and 200 or so by the bottle/can, with an emphasis on Portugal's rising scene and the freshest options from Europe, the USA and Canada. (www.facebook.com/OutroLadoLisboa)

Lux-Frágil
CLUB

22 MAP P82, H3

Lisbon's ice-cool, must-see club, Lux hosts big-name DJs spinning electro and house. It was started by late Lisbon nightlife impresario Manuel Reis and is part-owned by John Malkovich. Grab a spot on the terrace to see the sun rise over the Rio Tejo, or chill like a king or queen on the throne-like giant interior chairs. (www.luxfragil.com)

Entertainment

Senhor Fado
LIVE MUSIC

23 ⭐ MAP P82, G3

Small and lantern lit, this is a cosy spot for *fado vadio* (street fado). *Fadista* Ana Marina and guitarist Duarte Santos make a great double act. (www.sr-fado.com)

Tasca Bela
LIVE MUSIC

24 ⭐ MAP P82, G3

This intimate spot features live fado on Wednesday, Friday, Saturday and Sunday, and eclectic cultural fare (jazz, poetry readings) on other nights. Although there is a €19 minimum spend, unlike most fado houses you won't have to buy a pricey meal, as it's an appetisers-and-drinks kind of place. Fado begins at 9.30pm. (www.facebook.com/bela.vinhosepetiscos)

A Baiuca
LIVE MUSIC

25 ⭐ MAP P82, E5

On a good night, walking into A Baiuca is like gatecrashing a family party. It's a special place with *fado vadio*, where locals take a turn and spectators hiss if anyone dares to chat during the singing. There's a €25 minimum spend, which is as tough to swallow as the food, though the fado is spectacular. Reserve ahead.

Mesa de Frades
LIVE MUSIC

26 ⭐ MAP P82, F3

A magical place to hear fado, tiny Mesa de Frades used to be a chapel. It's tiled with exquisite

Portas do Sol

ONA JOURNEY/SHUTTERSTOCK ©

Mouraria, Alfama & Graça Entertainment

Fado

There is no better way to tune into the Portuguese psyche, some say, than by listening to fado: plaintive, bittersweet music overflowing with emotional intensity. Ask locals what fado means and you'll get a different answer every time. And indeed, the more you listen to it, the more you realise how diverse the genre is. As one *fadista* (singer of fado) sagely put it: 'Fado is life itself: happiness, sadness, poetry, history.'

The Origins of Fado

Fado's origins are largely traceable to the backstreets of working-class Alfama. The ditties of homesick sailors, the poetic ballads of the Moors, the bluesy songs of Brazilian slaves – all are cited as possible influences, and no doubt fado is a blend of these and more. Central to all forms of fado is *saudade*, a hard-to-translate, distinctly Portuguese concept redolent of nostalgic longing. This often underpins recurring themes in fado such as destiny (*fado* means 'fate'), remorse, heartbreak and loneliness. In Lisbon, fado typically consists of a solo vocalist singing to the accompaniment of a 12-stringed Portuguese guitar and viola.

Famous Fadistas

If fado was born in Alfama, it was Amália Rodrigues (1920–99) who took it to the world with her heartbreaking trills and poetic soul. The so-called Rainha do Fado (Queen of Fado) still holds a special place in the hearts of the Portuguese. More recently, *fadistas* have continued to broaden fado's scope and appeal – often adding a pinch of blues, a splash of Argentine tango or a dash of flamenco. The best known of the new generation *fadistas* is Mariza, whose 2007 *Concerto em Lisboa* and 2008 *Terra* albums received Latin Grammy nominations.

Fado in Alfama

Wander through Alfama today and you'll almost certainly hear the strains of fado drifting from open windows of clubs. Performances range from light-hearted *fado vadio*, a kind of jam session where amateurs take turns to sing, to fully blown professional acts. Which you prefer is a matter of taste. Wherever you go, when the lights go down, the audience falls silent – a sign of respect for the song of the soul.

azulejos and has just a handful of tables, including a dark and sexy mezzanine level. Shows begin at around 10.30pm. (www.facebook.com/mesadefradeslisboa)

Damas
LIVE MUSIC

27 ⭐ MAP P82, E1

Part restaurant, bar and alternative concert hall, Damas has given the cool kids a reason to climb the hill to Graça since opening in 2015. From DJs spinning electronica to African and indie rock bands, there's always an eclectic mix of sound here and it's often free. (www.facebook.com/pg/DAMASLISBOA)

VALSA
CONCERT VENUE

28 ⭐ MAP P82, D1

Founded by Brazilian-born Lisbon-based former musicians Nika (Mariana Serafim) and Marina Ginde, this cultural centre/bar/restaurant in Graça is also a safe haven and welcoming space for independent artists and members of the LGBTIQ+ community. It has a packed calendar of cultural events and workshops. (www.valsa.pt)

Shopping

Madalena à Janela
ARTS & CRAFTS

29 🔒 MAP P82, A4

Owned by two Portugal-based French childhood friends, this store is a tribute to their love for Portuguese-made arts and crafts. Browse (and buy) ethical and local ceramics, tote bags, and T-shirts.

XVIII Azulejo e Faiança
CERAMICS

30 🔒 MAP P82, D4

This store across the street from Miradouro de Santa Luzia (p81) specialises in hand-painted *azule-jos* produced using the same techniques of the 18th century. It's ideal for souvenir shoppers who want to take home an antique-looking one-of-a-kind piece. (www.xviii.pt)

Benamôr
COSMETICS

31 🔒 MAP P82, B6

Benamôr is a classic Portuguese brand dating to 1925, and its flag-ship store stocks hand and face creams and soaps in deliciously art-deco packaging. Their 'miracle' face cream hasn't changed one iota from 1925 and, like Claus Porto (p52), the brand is enjoying a 21st-century renaissance that has seen it evolve from an everyday product to a hipsterised retro cool must-have. (www.benamor1925.com)

Era Uma Vez Um Sonho
TOYS

32 🔒 MAP P82, C5

For over 20 years this colourful and enchanting shop has dealt in unique puppets, stuffed animals, puzzles and illustrated books, all handcrafted in Portugal and spawning a long list of in-country folklore characters. (www.eraumavezumsonho.pt)

Feira da Ladra
MARKET

33 🔒 MAP P82, G2

Browse and haggle for buried treasures at this massive flea market. You'll find old records, coins, baggy pants, dog-eared poetry books and other attic junk. Watch your wallet – it isn't called 'thieves market' for nothing. (www.cm-lisboa.pt)

Top Experience 📷
Tour Museu Nacional do Azulejo

When the queen Dona Leonor founded the Convento da Madre de Deus in 1509, she surely had no idea that the Manueline convent would one day become a stunning tribute to the azulejo (hand-painted tile). This exceptional museum unravels 500 years of Portuguese history and craftsmanship.

www.facebook.com/museunazulejo

Sala de Grande Vista de Lisboa

Tucked away on the 2nd floor, the early-18th-century Great View of Lisbon is the museum's undisputed highlight. Attributed to Spanish tile painter Gabriel del Barco, the huge panoramic panel beautifully encapsulates the city before the earthquake struck in 1755. Pick out Lisbon's seven hills, riverfront and landmarks past and present in the intricately painted blue-and-white *azulejos*.

Nossa Senhora da Vida

Made up of 1498 tiles, the late-16th-century Altarpiece of Our Lady of Life is one of Portugal's earliest *azulejo* masterpieces. Trompe l'œil diamond-tip tiles fringe the base, while ivy-clad columns frame erudite evangelists St John and St Luke, and the centrepiece scene showing the Adoration of the Shepherds.

Church

This Mannerist church in high baroque style is a breathtakingly lavish gilt, fresco and *azulejo* confection. Cherubs appear to flutter above the gilded altarpieces, and the ceiling is festooned with frescos depicting the life of the Virgin and Christ. Look for late-17th-century Dutch tile panels showing Moses and the Burning Bush, Franciscans at prayer and the Cortege of Shepherds.

Capela de Santo António

On the 1st floor, this chapel is a shrine to Franciscan preacher St Anthony of Lisbon. Commissioned by Dom João V, it's a stellar example of Portuguese baroque, with parquetry flooring, intricate wood carvings and a prized 18th-century terracotta crib. The blue-and-white *azulejo* panels show scenes from the life of hermit saints and the miracles of St Anthony.

★ **Top Tips**

○ The permanent collection is huge – allow two to three hours to do the museum justice.

○ Free English audio guides are available (and also for mobile phones).

○ Admission is free on Sunday until 2pm for Portuguese citizens/residents only.

○ Money-saving combo tickets are available with Panteão Nacional (€7), plus Museu Nacional de Arte Antiga (€15), among others.

✕ **Take a Break**

The **museum cafe** (snacks and mains are €5 to €9) is covered in 19th-century culinary *azulejos*. It opens onto a leafy courtyard and is an atmospheric place for a coffee and crêpe or a lunch special.

★ **Getting There**

Buses 759 and 728 from central Lisbon (Restauradores and Praça do Comércio).

Belém

In Belém, Atlantic breezes, nautical monuments and boats gliding along the wide Rio Tejo cast you back to those 'glory days' of the so-called Age of Discovery, when the world was Portugal's colonial oyster. And at dusk, when the crowds subside and the softening light paints the monastery's Manueline turrets gold, this riverside neighbourhood is yours alone for exploring.

The Short List

○ **Mosteiro dos Jerónimos (p96)** *Gazing upon the stunning Manueline cloisters inside this monastery.*

○ **Antiga Confeitaria de Belém (p105)** *Wallowing in the sweet satisfaction of a piping-hot, custard-cream-filled pastel de Belém.*

○ **Museu Coleção Berardo (p98)** *Getting your contemporary-art fix amid a world-class collection of abstract, surrealist and pop art.*

○ **Feitoria (p108)** *A Michelin-starred dining adventure at chef André Cruz' waterfront temple.*

Getting There & Around

🚋 The easiest, quickest and most scenic way to reach Belém from downtown Lisbon. Tram 15E runs from Praça da Figueira to Belém via Alcântara (around 30 minutes' journey). Tram 18 runs from Cais do Sodré to Ajuda.

🚌 Bus 728 operates frequently (several hourly) between Belém and central Lisbon, stopping at Praça do Comércio and Cais do Sodré.

🚆 The suburban Comboios de Portugal Cais do Sodré–Cascais train line runs from central Lisbon to Belém in eight minutes.

Belém Map on p102

Torre de Belém (p103) AMIRRAIZAT/SHUTTERSTOCK ©

Top Experience

Wander through 16th-century Mosteiro dos Jerónimos

Diogo de Boitaca's creative vision and Dom Manuel I's gold-laden coffers gave rise to this fantasy fairy tale of a monastery, founded in 1501 to trumpet Vasco da Gama's discovery of a sea route to India. Now a Unesco World Heritage Site, Jerónimos was once populated by monks whose spiritual job for four centuries was to comfort sailors and pray for the king's soul.

◎ MAP P102, C2

www.patrimoniocultural.gov.pt

Igreja Santa Maria de Belém

Entering the church through the western portal, you'll notice tree-trunk-like columns growing into the ceiling, itself a spiderweb of stone. Navigator Vasco da Gama is interred in the lower chancel, left of the entrance, opposite 16th-century poet Luís Vaz de Camões. From the upper choir is a superb view of the church.

Cloister

The honey-stone Manueline cloister drips with organic detail in its delicately scalloped arches, twisting turrets and columns intertwined with leaves, vines and knots. Pick out symbols of the age, like the armillary sphere and the cross of the Military Order, plus gargoyles and fantastical beasties on the upper level. In the north wing of the cloister, you'll find the tomb of Portugal's great literary figure Fernando Pessoa, whose remains were transferred here to a tomb by master sculptor Lagoa Henriques in 1985.

Chapter House & Refectory

Vines, flowers, cherubs and reliefs of St Jerome and St Bernard frame the Chapter House's 16th-century portal holding the tomb of Portuguese historian Alexandre Herculano. In the vaulted refectory, 18th-century *azulejo* (hand-painted tile) panels depict the miracle of the loaves and fishes, and scenes from the life of Joseph. António Campelo's evocative mural shows the Adoration of the Shepherds.

South Portal

The South Portal is the elaborate handiwork of 16th-century architect João de Castilho. The figure of Nossa Senhora de Belém (Our Lady of Bethlehem) sits surrounded by apostles, prophets and angels. Note Henry the Navigator, high on a pedestal, and scenes from the life of St Jerome above the door.

★ Top Tips

o Try to visit in the morning on clear days, when bright sunlight illuminates the church's stained-glass windows in a kaleidoscopic show of light.

o Save a few euros by getting the Lisboa Card, if you're planning to visit multiple attractions in Belém.

o Arrive early or late to appreciate the monastery at its serene best.

✖ Take a Break

Grab a *pastel de Belém* (custard tart) at nearby Antiga Confeitaria de Belém (p105) and enjoy it among the leafy environs of several gardens across the street from the monastery.

One of Lisbon's iconic vintage trams has been born again as the nicely chilled **Banana Cafe** (www.facebook.com/bananacafe.lisboa), with tables set up under the trees. It's a relaxed spot for a coffee, sangria or light snack.

Top Experience 📷

Muse Over Contemporary Art at the Museu Coleção Berardo

Bankrolled by billionaire art collector José Berardo, this gallery holds its own with the Tates and Guggenheims of this world. Yet, incredibly, it's still under the must-see sightseeing radar. Dadaism, minimalism, kinetic art, surrealism and conceptualism; works by Picasso, Warhol, Yves Klein, Pollock, Miró and Lichtenstein – this mind-blowing collection spans the spectrum of modern and contemporary art. Go. Go today.

◎ MAP P102, C3

www.museuberardo.pt

ARCHITECTS: VITTORIO GREGOTTI AND MANUEL SALGADO / MACBERMOKEY A / MM / LOCK DHOTO ©

British & American Pop Art

Race back to the 1950s and '60s contemplating pop-art masterpieces from both sides of the pond. Warhol's silk-screened portrait of Judy Garland, *Ten Foot Flowers*, *Brillo Box* tower and *Campbell's Soup* steal the limelight. Look too for David Hockney's *Picture Emphasising Stillness* and Lichtenstein's *Interior with Restful Paintings*.

Cubism & Dadaism

Several abstract pieces by Picasso, daddy of cubism, are on display, among them his early-20th-century *Tête de Femme* and *Femme dans un Fauteuil*. The anti-war Dadaists also sought to break with conventional art forms. Emblematic of the movement is French artist Marcel Duchamp's 1914 *Le Porte Bouteilles (Bottle Dryer)*.

Surrealism

Explore outlandish works by Man Ray, such as his mixed-media *Café Man Ray* and *Talking Picture*, and other standouts of the movement such as Magritte's spacey *Le Gouffre Argenté*, Joan Miró's *Figure à la Bougie*, Max Ernst's inky *Paysage Noir* and Jean Arp's teardrop-like *Feuilles Placées Selon les Lois du Hasard*. For a different perspective, zoom in on the monochromatic photography of Lisbon-born Fernando Lemos.

Modern & Contemporary Sculpture

Sculptures stopping you in your tracks by the entrance include Niki de Saint-Phalle's curvaceous, rainbow-bright *Les Baigneuses (Swimmers)*, Pedro Cabrita Reis' industrial-meets-abstract *Amarração*, and Joana Vasconcelos' green wine-bottle wonder, *Nectar*. Inside, look for bronze creations by Antony Gormley, Barry Flanagan and Henry Moore.

★ Top Tips

o Admission is free all day on Saturday.

o Pick up a free guide at the entrance for some background on the permanent exhibition.

o Visit the website for details of upcoming temporary exhibitions; these are held on level 0.

o Allow at least a couple of hours to do this gallery justice.

✖ Take a Break

Cross over to the riverside for a glass of wine and light snacks with a view at À Margem (p109).

Hidden down a small alley, a short walk away, cosy Taberna dos Ferreiros (p108) is a wonderful spot for modernised Portuguese fare.

Walking Tour 🥾

Belém's Age of Discovery

A stroll through nautical-flavoured Belém, with its broad river views and exuberant Manueline architecture, catapults you back to Portugal's so-called Age of Discovery – the 15th and 16th centuries, when seafarers like Vasco da Gama and Henry the Navigator set sail for lands rich in gold and spices aboard mighty caravels, and Portugal was but a drop in Dom Manuel I's colonial ocean.

Walk Facts

Start Praça do Império;
🚋15, 🚌728
Finish Torre de Belém;
🚋15, 🚌728
Length 2.5km; 1½ hours

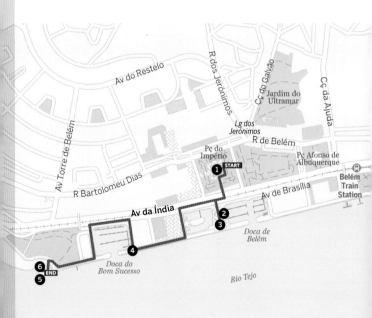

❶ Praça do Império

Even blasé locals never tire of the uplifting view of the **Mosteiro dos Jerónimos** (p96) and Rio Tejo from this stately plaza, set around a fountain and fringed by box hedges. Note the Age of Discovery symbols, such as anchors and the cross of the Military Order, featured in flowers and foliage. A controversial restoration process was set in motion in 2021 to turn these symbols of former Portuguese colonies into fixed cobblestone displays.

❷ Maritime Map

Head across to the breezy riverfront promenade, looking down as you approach the Padrão dos Descobrimentos, to spot a **mosaic map** charting the routes of Portuguese mariners and the dates of colonisation, from the Azores (1427) to Calcutta (1498) and beyond.

❸ Padrão dos Descobrimentos

Like a caravel caught in midswell, the 56m-high **Padrão dos Descobrimentos** (p104) depicts Henry the Navigator and some of the major figures of Portugal's maritime history. Take the lift (or puff up 267 steps) to the windswept *miradouro* for 360-degree views over the river.

❹ Doca do Bom Sucesso

Take a brisk walk along the riverfront to the Doca do Bom Sucesso, where you can watch the boats and seagulls over drinks at waterfront **Bar 38° 41'** (p109). Belém's waterfront is prime people-watching real estate for locals and tourists alike. Alternatively, this is a relaxed spot to dip into Luís Vaz de Camões' *The Lusiads*, an epic poem recounting Vasco da Gama's voyages.

❺ Torre de Belém

Feel the pull of the past and the breezes of the Atlantic as you gaze up at the Torre de Belém, an early-16th-century icon of the Age of Discovery and a prime example of whimsical Manueline style with its ribbed cupolas.

❻ Hidden Rhino

It's easy to miss one of Torre de Belém's most intriguing features. Below the western tower is a rhinoceros, a **stone carving** of the Indian rhino Manuel I shipped to Pope Leo X as a token of his esteem in 1515. The rhino never reached Rome – it drowned when the ship capsized – but Albrecht Dürer immortalised it in his famous woodcut.

Belém

Bike Iberia (4.5km)

AJUDA

Palácio Nacional da Ajuda ⦿ 4

Tv da Memória

R General João Almeida

Cc da Ajuda

Jardim do Ultramar

Museu da Presidência da República

Antigo Picadeiro Real

R do Embaixador

R da Junqueira

Av da India

Quake ⦿ 10

Museu de Arte, Arquitetura e Tecnologia

⦿ 3 ✕ 15

⦿ 19

Jardim Botânico Tropical

Cc do Galvão

✕ 6

✕ 5

✕ 14

Pç Afonso de Albuquerque ⦿ 1

Museu Nacional dos Coches

Belém Train Station

Av de Brasília

R de Belém

✕ 11 ✕ 16

⦿ 7

Lg dos Jerónimos

Mosteiro dos Jerónimos ⦿

R dos Jerónimos

BELÉM

Museu de Marinha ⦿ 9

Pç do Império

Av da India

Doca de Belém

Padrão dos Descobrimentos

Av de Brasília

⦿ 8

Rio Tejo

R Dom Lourenço de Almeida

R Bartolomeu Dias

✕ 12 ⦿ 24

⦿ 23 ⦿ 22

Museu Coleção Berardo

⦿ 18 ✕ 20

✕ 21

Doca do Bom-Sucesso

Av do Restelo

R Dom Francisco de Almeida

R São Francisco Xavier ⦿ 13

R Tristão da Cunha

R Dom Cristóvão da Gama

Av Torre de Belém

R Pedrouços

Torre de Belém ⦿ 2

Av da India

✕ 17

N ⦿

0 500 m
0 0.25 miles

Sights

Museu Nacional dos Coches
MUSEUM

1 ◎ MAP P102, E3

Cinderella wannabes delight in Portugal's most visited museum, which dazzles with its world-class collection of 70 17th- to 19th-century coaches in an ultramodern (and some might say inappropriately contrasting) space that debuted in 2015. Don't miss Pope Clement XI's stunning ride, the scarlet-and-gold *Coach of the Oceans*, or the old royal riding school, Antigo Picadeiro Real (p104), across the street. (www.museudoscoches.gov.pt/pt)

Torre de Belém
TOWER

2 ◎ MAP P102, A4

Jutting out onto the Rio Tejo, this Unesco World Heritage–listed fortress epitomises the Age of Discovery. You'll need to breathe in to climb the narrow spiral staircase to the tower, which affords sublime views over Belém and the river. (www.patrimoniocultural.gov.pt)

Museu de Arte, Arquitetura e Tecnologia
MUSEUM

3 ◎ MAP P102, F3

Lisbon's latest riverfront star is this low-rise, glazed-tiled structure that intriguingly hips and sways into ground-level exhibition halls. Visitors can walk over and under its reflective surfaces, which play

Belém Sights

Museu Nacional dos Coches

TRABANTOS/SHUTTERSTOCK ©

with water, light and shadow, and pay homage to the city's intimate relationship with the sea. (MAAT; Art, Architecture & Technology Museum; www.maat.pt)

Palácio Nacional da Ajuda

PALACE

4 ◉ MAP P102, E1

Built in the early 19th century, this staggering neoclassical palace served as the royal residence from the 1860s until the end of the monarchy (1910). You can tour private apartments and state rooms, getting an eyeful of gilded furnishings and exquisite artworks dating back five centuries, as well as the queen's chapel, home to Portugal's only El Greco painting. It's a long uphill walk from Belém, or you can take tram 18E or several buses from downtown, including 760 from Praça do Comércio. (www.patrimoniocultural.gov.pt)

Antigo Picadeiro Real

MUSEUM

5 ◉ MAP P102, E2

Lisbon's original coach museum is now home to just seven of these majestic 18th-century four-wheeled works of art, but it's worth also visiting the stuccoed, frescoed halls of the former royal riding stables built by Italian architect Giacomo Azzolini in 1726 – a far more fitting and palatial rest home than the modern monolith, Museu Nacional dos Coches (p103), across the street. (Old Royal Riding School; www.museudoscoches. gov.pt/pt)

Museu da Presidência da República

MUSEUM

6 ◉ MAP P102, D2

Portugal's small presidential museum is worth a look for its fascinating state gifts exhibit – note the outrageous 1957 offering from Brazil's Juscelino Kubitschek, a massive tortoiseshell depicting hand-painted Brazilian scenes, plus Saudi swords and a gorgeous traditional Japanese dance scene. Don't miss the official presidential portrait of Mário Soares, either – that guy looked like fun! (Museum of the Presidency of the Republic; www. museu.presidencia.pt)

Jardim Botânico Tropical

GARDENS

7 ◉ MAP P102, D2

Far from the madding crowd, these botanical gardens bristle with hundreds of species, from date palms to monkey-puzzle trees. Spread across seven hectares, it's a peaceful, shady retreat on a sweltering summer's day. A highlight is the Macau garden, complete with mini pagoda, where bamboo rustles and a cool stream trickles. (www.museus.ulisboa.pt)

Padrão dos Descobrimentos

MUSEUM

8 ◉ MAP P102, C3

The monolithic Padrão dos Descobrimentos, looking like a caravel ship frozen in midswell, was inaugurated in 1960 on the 500th anniversary of Henry the Navigator's death. The 56m-high limestone giant is chock-full of Portuguese bigwigs. At the prow is Henry, while behind him are seafarers Vasco da Gama, Diogo Cão, Fernão de Magalhães (Ferdinand Magellan) and 29 other figures. (Discoveries Monument; www.padraodosdescobrimentos.pt)

Museu de Marinha
MUSEUM

9 MAP P102, C2

The Museu de Marinha is a nautical flashback to the Age of Discovery, with its armadas of model ships, cannonballs and shipwreck booty. Dig for buried treasure such as Vasco da Gama's portable wooden altar, 17th-century globes (note Australia's absence) and the polished private quarters of UK-built royal yacht *Amélia*. A separate building houses royal barges, 19th-century firefighting machines and seaplanes. (Naval Museum; http://ccm.marinha.pt/pt/museu)

Quake
MUSEUM

10 MAP P102, E3

Feel the floor shake at this immersive museum dedicated to Lisbon's 1755 earthquake. Upon arrival, visitors receive an identification wristband that can be scanned to check in and take pictures at selected spots. The two-hour experience takes you back in time, following a series of interactive rooms, until you reach the big earthquake simulator inside a replicated church. (www.lisbonquake.com)

Eating

Antiga Confeitaria de Belém
PASTRIES €

11 MAP P102, D2

Since 1837 this patisserie has been transporting locals to sugar-coated nirvana with heavenly *pastéis de Belém*. The crisp pastry nests are filled with custard cream, baked at 200°C for that perfect golden crust, then lightly dusted with cinnamon. Admire *azulejos* in the vaulted rooms or devour a still-warm tart at the counter and try to guess the secret ingredient. (Pastéis de Belém; www.pasteisdebelem.pt)

Pastéis de Belém

The origins of heavenly *pastéis de Belém* (aka *pastéis de nata*) stretch back to an early-19th-century sugar-cane refinery next to the Mosteiro dos Jerónimos. The liberal revolution swept through Portugal in 1820 and by 1834 all monasteries had been shut down, the monks expelled. Desperate to survive, some clerics saw the light in all that sugar, and *pastéis de Belém* were born. The top-secret custard tart recipe hasn't changed since then and shall forever serve as a reminder that calories need not be sinful. Amen.

The Age of Discovery

The 15th and 16th centuries were Portugal's so-called 'golden age', when the small kingdom built itself into a massive imperial power and Europe's wealthiest monarchy. Dom João I set the ball rolling when he conquered Ceuta, Morocco, in 1415. It was a turning point in Portuguese history. During this so-called Age of Discovery, seafaring Europeans made use of improved ships to navigate the globe, marking the beginning of a long period of imperialism and colonialism.

Manueline Riches

Portugal's biggest breakthrough came in 1497 during the reign of Manuel I, when Vasco da Gama reached southern India. With spices from the East and gold from Africa, as well as slaves, Portugal was soon rolling in monetary riches. Manuel I was so thrilled with the new wealth that he ordered a frenzied building spree. Top of his list was the Mosteiro dos Jerónimos in Belém, later to become his pantheon.

Enter Spain

Spain had also jumped on the power-hungry bandwagon and was soon disputing Portuguese claims. Christopher Columbus' 1492 arrival in America led to a fresh outburst of jealous conflict. It was resolved by the pope in the 1494 Treaty of Tordesillas, which divided the world between the two great powers along a line 370 leagues west of Cape Verde.

Epic Voyage

The rivalry spurred the first circumnavigation of the world. In 1519 Portuguese navigator Fernão de Magalhães (Ferdinand Magellan), his allegiance transferred to Spain after a tiff with Manuel I, set off to prove the Spice Islands (Moluccas) lay in Spanish 'territory'. He perished in the Philippines in 1521 but one of his ships reached the islands and then sailed home via the Cape of Good Hope, proving the earth was round.

Sinking Ship

By the 1570s, the huge cost of expeditions and an empire was taking its toll. Dom Sebastião's mortal defeat at the 1578 Battle of Alcácer-Quibir launched a downward spiral. When his successor, Cardinal Henrique, died in 1580, Felipe II of Spain fought for and won the throne. This marked the end of centuries of independence and Portugal's 'glorious' moment on the world stage.

Gelato Davvero GELATO €

12 MAP P102, C3

It's now worth tucking into Centro Cultural de Belém for something other than performances and contemporary art: 22 flavours of Lisbon's best Roman-style gelato lie in wait at Gelato Davvero. Filippo Licitra's creations often push the envelope – avocado, salmon, curried mango – but all the classics are here as well. There's another location near **Cais do Sodré**. (www.facebook.com/gelatodavvero)

Pastelaria Restelo BAKERY €

13 MAP P102, A2

Better known as Pastelaria O Careca ('The Bald Guy') among locals, this simple *pastelaria* flanking a small plaza has been dishing out Lisbon's sweetest croissants since 1954. It's definitely worth heading a few blocks inland from the tourist onslaught along Belém's waterfront for the doughy, sugar-coated goodness. (www.pastelariaocareca.pt)

Alecrim & Manjerona CAFE €

14 MAP P102, E2

Tucked away from the crowds on a side street, Alecrim & Manjerona ('Rosemary & Marjoram') is a cute grocery store, cafe, deli and wine bar rolled into one. Besides delicious homemade cakes and tarts, it rustles up wallet-friendly specials – from quiches to *bacalhau espiritual* (codfish gratin). (www.facebook.com/alecrimmanjeronamercearia)

Belém Eating

Pastéis de Belém (p105)

BRASILNUT1/GETTY IMAGES ©

Biking the Tejo

Lisbon is redefining itself with new biking/jogging paths. Coursing along the Rio Tejo for nearly 7km, the older path connects Cais do Sodré with Belém, passing ageing warehouses converted into open-air cafes, restaurants, nightspots and the Museu de Arte, Arquitetura e Tecnologia (MAAT); while the newest path extends 5km from Belém to the Fortress of Caxias. You may also ride upstream, connecting Santa Apolónia with Parque das Nações, an additional 8km jaunt. Rent wheels at any **Gira** (p149) bike station or from **Bike Iberia** (p149) near Cais do Sodré, which also produces the indispensable Lisbon Bike Map (€7).

Maat Café & Kitchen   CAFE €€

15   MAP P102, F3

After touring the exhibits at Museu de Arte, Arquitetura e Tecnologia (MAAT), you can refuel at the museum's café and restaurant overlooking the river. The café serves light snacks, such as sandwiches and wraps, while the restaurant offers a fusion of fine-dining dishes like duck magret in smoked teriyaki or truffled mushroom risotto. Brunch is also served on weekends, with special deals for kids. (www.mercantina.pt/maat-kitchen)

Taberna dos Ferreiros   PORTUGUESE €€

16   MAP P102, D2

Tucked away in a small street behind Belém's Jardim Botânico Tropical, this cosy tavern mixes classic Portuguese dishes with international influences. Try the house recipe of *bacalhau à Ferreiro* (codfish topped with a fried egg), or crispy tuna served with pineapple.

Darwin's Café   CAFE €€€

17   MAP P102, A4

This trendy, design-forward, evolution-themed cafe suffers from a bit of scholarly overreach inside (though the big, round banquettes are great for groups), but its elevated terrace affords postcard-perfect views of the Rio Tejo and Torre de Belém. It draws a fashion-forward local crowd with sophisticated pastas, risottos and the like, as well as an extensive list of bubbly by the flute. (www.darwincafe.com)

Feitoria   MODERN PORTUGUESE €€€

18   MAP P102, B4

A defining dining experience awaits at chef André Cruz' slick, contemporary, Michelin-starred restaurant overlooking the riverfront. Rich textures and seasonal ingredients dominate throughout four tasting menus (vegetarian options included), which showcase Portugal's rich and vibrant bounty. (www.restaurantefeitoria.com)

SUD Lisboa
Terrazza ITALIAN €€€

19 ⊗ MAP P102, F3

This hot riverside spot combines nicely with an afternoon visiting the MAAT next door. Upscale Italian is served with contemporary Portuguese-influenced dishes (low temperature codfish with clam cream sauce) alongside a design-forward space highlighted by a coconut-strewn bamboo ceiling. Cocktails (€12 to €19) also go down nicely on the plush patio. (www.sudlisboa.com)

Drinking

À Margem FUSION

20 🍷 MAP P102, B4

Well-positioned near the river's edge, this small, sun-drenched cube of glass and white stone boasts an open patio and large windows facing the Tejo and dramatic sunsets over the Torre de Belém. Locals come for fresh salads, cheese plates, bruschetta and other light bites (salads €12 to €14.50) that go nicely with a sundowner (wines €4 to €7.10). (www.amargem.com)

Bar 38° 41' BAR

21 🍷 MAP P102, B4

Watch boats bob on the water over coffee or cocktails (€9 to €13) at this stylish, dressed-in-black dockside lounge bar. Guest DJs liven things up on weekends in summer. (www.altishotels.com)

Entertainment

Centro Cultural
de Belém THEATRE

22 🌟 MAP P102, C3

The CCB presents a diverse programme spanning experimental jazz, contemporary ballet, boundary-crossing plays and performances by the Portuguese Chamber Orchestra. Buy tickets at the box office (open 11am to 8pm). (CCB; www.ccb.pt)

Shopping

Hangar Design Store DESIGN

23 🔒 MAP P102, C3

Fittingly located at the back of the CCB, where this discerning shop's Portuguese owner has assembled a well-curated collection of top design-forward objects from Portugal and beyond. (www.hangar.pt)

Portugal Manual ARTS & CRAFTS

24 🔒 MAP P102, C3

Even if you're not catching a show at CCB, it's worth stepping inside the ticket office to visit this creative pop-up store. Young Portuguese artisans are highlighted here on the shelves with their ceramics, textiles and other handmade creations. A slightly bigger collection is available at the Depozito store in Intendente. (www.portugalmanual.com)

Parque das Nações

A shining model of urban regeneration, Parque das Nações has almost single-handedly propelled the city into the 21st century since Expo '98. Glittering high-rises, sci-fi concert halls, a large aquarium and Europe's second longest bridge rise above a river so wide it could be the sea. This is the Lisbon of the future.

The Short List

○ **Oceanário de Lisboa (p112)** Diving into the underwater world of Europe's largest indoor aquarium, a conservation-conscious oceanarium that captivates all ages.

○ **Ponte Vasco da Gama (p116)** Ogling Europe's longest bridge at sunset, a no-filter-necessary cable-stayed stunner across the Rio Tejo.

○ **Casa Bota Feijão (p116)** Dunking juicy, spit-roasted suckling pig into peppery garlic sauce at this simple local favourite.

○ **Gare do Oriente (p115)** Pondering the best photo angles at Santiago Calatrava's Gothic-influenced, space-age train station.

Getting There & Around

Ⓜ The red line speeds you between central Lisbon and Oriente in around 20 minutes; services run frequently.

🚍 Services connecting Parque das Nações to central Lisbon include the 708 to Martim Moniz (via the airport, which is just three metro stops from Oriente).

Parque das Nações Map on p114

Top Experience 📷

Marvel at Marine Life at the Oceanário

Europe's largest indoor aquarium is an eye-popping pool of 8000 marine creatures splashing in 7 million litres of seawater. Sand tiger sharks, stingrays, pufferfish and sunfish swim in the mammoth central tank, while puffins, penguins and sea otters are featured in North Atlantic, Antarctic, Pacific and Indian Ocean marine-life exhibitions. Conservation is the name of the game.

◉ MAP P114, C4

www.oceanario.pt

Pacific Sea Otters

Make for the Pacific to coo over the Oceanário's superstar sea otters: Micas, Odi and Kasi. The trio are ridiculously cute as they turn somersaults, swim placidly on their backs and groom their fur.

Central Tank

Standing in front of this whopper of a tank, or 'global ocean', is like scuba diving without getting wet. Speckled zebra sharks, globular sunfish, shoals of neon fish and manta rays – the flying carpets of the underwater world – hold audiences captive.

Sleeping with the Sharks

Who needs bedtime stories when you can scare your kids (and maybe yourself) silly by sleeping next to a shark tank? Costing €60 per person, these midnight *Jaws* encounters zoom in on conservation and give you the run of the almost-empty Oceanário the next morning.

Penguins on Ice

Watch Magellanic and crested rockhopper penguins waddle and slide across the ice in the Antarctic exhibition, then go down to the subaquatic level to glimpse them swimming gracefully underwater.

Underwater Close-Ups

Ghost-like moon jellyfish, giant octopuses, lacy sea dragons and big-belly seahorses are among the more unusual species splashing around in the tanks on the subaquatic level. Geeky fact for Nemo fans: clownfish are transsexual, with the dominant male eventually morphing into a female.

★ Top Tips

o Buy tickets online to jump the queue.

o Join a backstage tour for insights into what goes on behind the scenes.

o Don't use the flash on your camera – it frightens the fish.

o Pick up an audio guide for a running commentary of the exhibition.

o Plan your visit around feeding times: sea otters 10am, 12.45pm and 3.15pm; penguins 10am and 3pm; manta rays and sunfish 12:30pm; sharks 10.30am Monday and Friday; stingrays 11.15am Monday, Wednesday and Friday.

✕ Take a Break

The pizzeria Zero-Zero (p116), one of Lisbon's best, sits just across the street from the aquarium.

For impressive Rio Tejo and Ponte Vasco da Gama views, imbibe a cocktail at River Lounge (p117) at the other end of Parque das Nações.

Parque das Nações

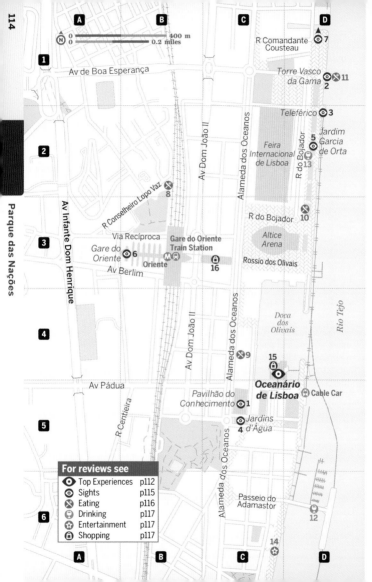

N
0 ————— 400 m
0 ————— 0.2 miles

R Comandante Cousteau ⊙ 7

Av de Boa Esperança

Torre Vasco da Gama ⊙⊗ 11
2

Teleférico ⊙ 3

Av Dom João II

Alameda dos Oceanos

Feira Internacional de Lisboa

Jardim Garcia de Orta
5
R do Bojador
13

R do Bojador ⊗ 10

Av Conselheiro Lopo Vaz ⊗ 8

Via Recíproca

Gare do Oriente Train Station

Gare do Oriente ⊙ 6

Oriente Ⓜ

Av Berlim

Altice Arena

Rossio dos Olivais

🔒 16

Av Infante Dom Henrique

Av Dom João II

Alameda dos Oceanos

Doca dos Olivais

Rio Tejo

⊗ 9

15 🔒

Oceanário de Lisboa ⊙

⊕ Cable Car

Av Pádua

R Centieira

Pavilhão do Conhecimento ⊙ 1

Alameda dos Oceanos

Jardins d'Água ⊙ 4

Passeio do Adamastor

12

14 ✪

For reviews see
⊙ Top Experiences p112
⊙ Sights p115
⊗ Eating p116
🍷 Drinking p117
✪ Entertainment p117
🔒 Shopping p117

Sights

Pavilhão do Conhecimento
MUSEUM

1 ⊙ MAP P114, C5

Kids won't grumble about science at the interactive Pavilhão do Conhecimento, where they can run riot in the adult-free unfinished house, get dizzy on a high-wire bicycle or have fun whipping up tornadoes and blowing massive soap bubbles. (Pavilion of Knowledge; www.pavconhecimento.pt)

Torre Vasco da Gama
LANDMARK

2 ⊙ MAP P114, D1

No, that's not Dubai! Shaped like the sail of navigator Vasco da Gama's caravel, this 145m-high, concrete-and-steel skyscraper was designed by architects Leonor Janeiro and Nick Jacobs. Sidling up to the tower is the slick, five-star **Myriad by Sana Hotels** (www.myriad.pt), which opened in 2013 and bears the hallmark of architect Nuno Leónidas. Note that the tower is closed to the public, that is unless you have a reservation for its Michelin-star restaurant Fifty Seconds (p116).

Teleférico
CABLE CAR

3 ⊙ MAP P114, D2

Hitch a ride on this 20m-high cable car, linking Torre Vasco da Gama to the Oceanário. The ride affords bird's-eye views across Parque das Nações' skyline and the glittering Rio Tejo that will have you burning up the pixels on your camera. (Telecabine Lisboa; www.telecabinelisboa.pt)

Jardins d'Água
WATER PARK

4 ⊙ MAP P114, C5

These free, themed water gardens are a great spot to cool off in summer. When the sun shines, parents and their overexcited kids get soaked ducking behind the raging waterfalls and misty geysers, and testing out the hands-on water activities. (Water Gardens; www.cm-lisboa.pt/equipamentos/equipamento/info/jardins-da-agua-parque-das-nacoes)

Jardim Garcia de Orta
GARDENS

5 ⊙ MAP P114, D2

Bristling with exotic foliage from Portugal's former colonies, the Jardim Garcia de Orta is named after a 16th-century Portuguese naturalist and pioneer in tropical medicine. Botanical rarities include Madeira's bird of paradise and serpentine dragon tree. (www.cm-lisboa.pt/equipamentos/equipamento/info/jardim-garcia-de-orta)

Gare do Oriente
ARCHITECTURE

6 ⊙ MAP P114, B3

Designed by acclaimed Spanish architect Santiago Calatrava, the space-age Gare do Oriente is an extraordinary vaulted structure, with slender columns fanning out into a concertina roof to create a kind of geometric crystalline forest. (Oriente Station)

Ponte Vasco da Gama BRIDGE

7 MAP P114, D1

Vanishing into a watery distance, the Ponte Vasco da Gama is Europe's second longest bridge, stretching 17.2km across the Rio Tejo. (www.lusoponte.pt)

Eating

Casa Bota Feijão PORTUGUESE €

8 MAP P114, B2

Don't be fooled by the nondescript decor and railroad-track views – when a tucked-away place is this crowded with locals at lunchtime midweek, it must be doing something right. Everyone's here for one thing and one thing only: Bairrada-style *leitão* – suckling pig spit-roasted on an open fire until juicy and meltingly tender, doused in a beautiful, peppery garlic sauce.

ZeroZero PIZZA €€

9 MAP P114, C4

This location of top pizzeria ZeroZero is a modern, industrial-chic affair. Inside, a massive wall of firewood fuels the wood-burning ovens, which churn out favourites like 18-month prosciutto *de parma* with mushrooms or *fior di latte* mozzarella, porcini, asiago cheese and black truffle cream. Outside, a large and airy patio is a fine retreat from Parque das Nações. (www.pizzeriazerozero.pt)

Old House CHINESE €€€

10 MAP P114, D3

Transport yourself to China at this authentic Szechuan power-house (tamed for local tastes), an upscale Chinese chain restaurant that chose Parque das Nações for its first foray outside the motherland. The daunting list of specialities, including Beijing duck (whole €57.50), hotpots (the veggie version with noodled tofu is outstanding) and plenty of garlic- and pepper-loaded dishes, is a welcome taste-bud change-up. (www.theoldhouseportugal.pt)

Fifty Seconds GASTRONOMY €€€

This upscale panoramic restaurant (see **2** Map p114, D1) gets its name from the time it takes the lift to whisk foodies up the 120m-high

---

Street Art & Culinary Ventures 💬

Dynamic Parque das Nações has so much exciting architecture, art and gastronomy to offer and is a must-visit. I especially love the evolving creative scene on the edge of the Rio Tejo – from tasting the best contemporary Portuguese cuisine at José Avillez' Cantinho do Avillez to admiring Bordalo II's incredible giant Iberian Lynx art installation, made entirely of rubbish and plastic.

Recommended by Chitra Stern, *founder of Martinhal Resorts @martinhal*

Vasco de Gama Tower at the Myriad by Sana Hotel. Superstar chef Martín Berasategui masterfully marries Basque-grounded fusion with Portuguese ingredients – cod brandade with manzanilla and yuzu mayo, suckling lamb with parmesan cheese and smoked aubergine puree. (www.fiftyseconds experience.com)

River Lounge MEDITERRANEAN €€€

11 ✖ MAP P114, D1

This slinky, monochrome, glass-walled restaurant-lounge ups the style ante in Parque das Nações. Med-inspired cuisine is given a light touch of sophistication in dishes such as grilled stone bass with *pata negra* (Iberian ham). Good cocktails (€15 to €20) are perfect for pre-or post-dinner drinks, and the terrace has stunning views of the Rio Tejo and Ponte Vasco da Gama. (www.myriad.pt)

Drinking

Bliss Bar BAR

12 🍺 MAP P114, D6

This terrace bar overlooking the marina serves beers and cocktails until the wee hours. Pair it with one of their giant toasts, or share some nachos with your mates. (www. facebook.com/BlissBarExpo)

Irish & Co IRISH PUB

13 🍺 MAP P114, D2

This double-decker chain pub is the liveliest drinking den along

the waterfront. There's typical homesick-remedying pub fare, several beers, including Guinness, Kilkenny, Carlsberg and some of Super Bock's more crafty attempts, are on draught. A suspended biplane hovers above the large patio (though water views are partially blocked by shrubbery). (www.irishco.pt)

Entertainment

Teatro Camões BALLET

14 ⭐ MAP P114, C6

Teatro Camões is home to the Portuguese National Ballet Company, which is under the artistic direction of Paulo Ribeiro. (www.cnb.pt/teatro-camoes)

Shopping

Oceanário de Lisboa Store GIFTS & SOUVENIRS

15 🔒 MAP P114, C4

Oceanário de Lisboa's 600-sq-metre eco-focused museum shop stocks clothes, souvenirs, cuddly toys and more, and has partnerships with local producers and craft workers. (https://loja.ocean ario.pt)

Centro Vasco da Gama MALL

16 🔒 MAP P114, C3

A glass-roofed mall sheltering high-street stores, a cinema and food court – upper-level restaurants have outdoor seating with views. (www.centrovascodagama.pt)

Explore ⊚

Marquês de Pombal, Rato & Saldanha

Some of Lisbon's finest restaurants, designer boutiques and concert halls make it easy to fill an entire day in this northern swath of the city. Beyond the tree-fringed Avenida da Liberdade lie graceful art-nouveau houses, manicured gardens and galleries showcasing artists from Paula Rego to Rembrandt. High culture and good living are what these modern neighbourhoods are all about.

The Short List

○ **Museu Calouste Gulbenkian – Coleção do Fundador (p120)** Ogling a world-class collection of Western and Eastern art at this outstanding museum.

○ **Mãe d'Água (p124)** Wandering part of the city's astonishing 18th-century aqueduct system.

○ **Red Frog (p128)** Drinking in a sophisticated world of mixology at one of Lisbon's top spots for a tipple.

○ **Parque Eduardo VII (p124)** Frolicking amid manicured lawns at Lisbon's centrepiece green space.

Getting There & Around

Ⓜ Attractions are spread out, but the metro is a breeze. Handy stops on the yellow and blue lines: Avenida, Marquês de Pombal, Rato, São Sebastião and Parque. If you're visiting more than one place, invest in a 24-hour Carris/metro pass.

🚌 The 744 stops at Marquês de Pombal and Avenida da Liberdade en route to and from Lisbon's airport.

Marquês de Pombal, Rato & Saldanha Map on p122

Parque Eduardo VII (p124) SERGII FIGURNYI/SHUTTERSTOCK ©

Top Experience 📷

Immerse Yourself in Art at Museu Calouste Gulbenkian

The Museu Calouste Gulbenkian showcases an epic collection of Western and Eastern art that's famous for its outstanding quality and breadth. You can easily spend half a day taking a chronological tour of the treasures that wealthy Armenian art collector Calouste Sarkis Gulbenkian (1869–1955) picked up on his world travels – this is an exuberant feast of fine and decorative arts.

◎ MAP P122, C1

Founder's Collection

www.gulbenkian.pt

Dutch & Flemish Masters

Old Master enthusiasts are in their element contemplating 17th-century masterpieces such as Rembrandt's chiaroscuro *Portrait of an Old Man* and Rubens' frantic *Loves of the Centaurs* and biblical *Flight into Egypt*. Ruisdael's stormy Norwegian scenes and Van Dyck portraits star among other highlights.

René Lalique

An entire room spotlights the impossibly intricate glassware and jewellery of French art-nouveau designer René Lalique. Marvel at his naturalistic diadems, hair combs, chalices and bracelets, bejewelled with baroque pearls and opals.

19th-Century Fine Art

This collection zooms in on French and English masterpieces such as Manet's *Boy Blowing Bubbles,* Monet's *Break-Up of the Ice* and Turner's *Wreck of a Transport Ship*. Look, too, for Impressionistic Degas portraits, Théodore Rousseau landscapes and Rodin's *Eternal Spring* sculpture.

Egyptian & Greco-Roman Art

With its gilded mummy mask, bronze cats and bas-relief pharaohs, the Egyptian collection provides a fascinating insight into this chapter of history. Next is the Greco-Roman room, displaying Greek coins and medallions, Roman glass and ceramics.

Islamic Art

Be captivated by the rich hues and geometric patterns of the museum's Persian carpets, kilims and brocaded silk – many dating to the 15th and 16th centuries. These feature alongside Ottoman faience, ornate tiles and Egyptian mosque lamps.

★ Top Tips

◦ Visit on Sunday after 2pm when entry to the permanent collection is free.

◦ Guided English private group tours (€10) are available for booking.

◦ Check the website for special events aimed at kids and families.

◦ Learn more about the works on display with an audio guide.

✕ Take a Break

For something sweet, take a stroll to nearby Versailles (p125), a gloriously old-world patisserie.

The food court Gourmet Experience (p126) at El Corte Inglés dishes up fantastic and quick meals from Michelin-starred Iberian chefs, including José Avillez and Henrique Sá Pessoa.

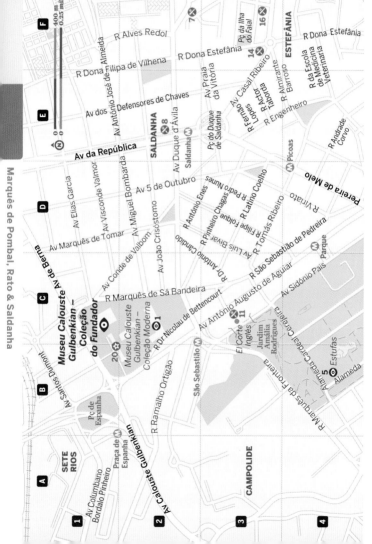

Marquês de Pombal, Rato & Saldanha

SETE RIOS

Av Columbano Bordalo Pinheiro

Praça de Espanha

Av Calouste Gulbenkian

Pç de Espanha

R Ramalho Ortigão

CAMPOLIDE

São Sebastião

R Dr Nicolau de Bettencourt

Museu Calouste Gulbenkian – Coleção Moderna

Museu Calouste Gulbenkian – Coleção do Fundador

Av de Berna

Av Santos Dumont

Av Elias Garcia

Av Visconde Valmor

Av Marquês de Tomar

Av Conde de Valbom

Av Miguel Bombarda

Av João Crisóstomo

R Marquês de Sá Bandeira

Av 5 de Outubro

Av da República

Av dos Defensores de Chaves

R António José de Almeida

R Dona Filipa de Vilhena

R Alves Redol

SALDANHA

Pç do Duque de Saldanha

Saldanha

Av Duque d'Ávila

Av Praia da Vitória

R Dona Estefânia

Pç da Ilha do Faial

ESTEFÂNIA

R Dona Estefânia

R da Escola de Medicina Veterinária

Av Casal Ribeiro

R Fernão Lopes

R Actor Taborda

R Almirante Barroso

R Engenheiro

R Andrade Corvo

Picoas

Pereira de Melo

R Viriato

R António Enes

Pç Pedro Nunes

R Pinheiro Chagas

R Latino Coelho

R Filipe Folque

Av Luís Bívar

R Tomás Ribeiro

R São Sebastião de Pedreira

Av São Sebastião de Aguiar

Av António Augusto de Aguiar

Av Sidónio Pais

Parque

El Corte Inglés

Jardim Amália Rodrigues

Al Cardeal Cerejeira

R Marquês da Fronteira

Estufas

Al Cardeal Cerejeira

Alameda

400 m
0.25 miles

N

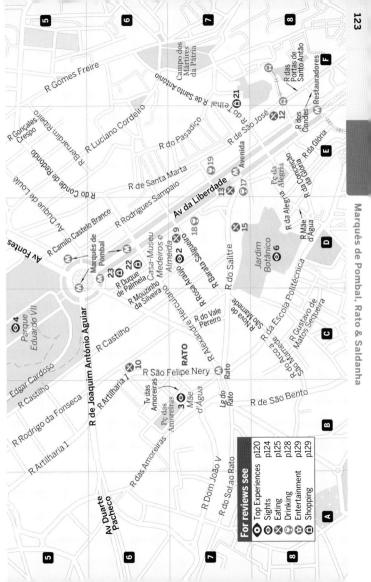

Marquês de Pombal, Rato & Saldanha

Map labels:

R Gomes Freire

R Gonçalves Crespo

R do Conde de Redondo

AV Duque de Loule

R Bernardim Ribeiro

R Luciano Cordeiro

Campo dos Mártires da Pátria

R de Santo António

R do Telhal

R de São José ❸ ㉑

R das Portas de Santo Antão

R do Pasadiço

R de Santa Marta

R Rodrigues Sampaio

R Camilo Castelo Branco

R dos Condes

Ⓜ Restauradores

R da Glória

R da Conceição da Glória

Pç da Alegria

R da Alegria

❶⑲

Av da Liberdade

⑰ ⑬ ❸

Avenida Ⓜ

R Mãe d'Agua

Marquês de Pombal Ⓜ

Ⓜ ⑱ Ⓜ ❾

Casa-Museu Medeiros e Almeida

R Braancamp

R Rosa Araújo

Jardim Botânico ❻

R da Escola Politécnica

❸ ⑮

㉓ ⑳Ⓜ

R Duque de Palmela

R Mouzinho da Silveira

R Alexandre Herculano

R Nova de São Mamede

R do Salitre

R do Vale Pereiro

R Gustavo de Matos Sequeira

R do Arco a São Mamede

AV Fontes

Ⓜ ❹

Parque Eduardo VII

Edgar Cardoso

R Castilho

R Rodrigo da Fonseca

R Castilho

R de Joaquim António Aguiar

R Artilharia 1

❸ ⑩

Tv das Amoreiras

Pç das Amoreiras

❸ Mãe d'Agua

R São Felipe Nery

RATO

Lg do Rato

Ⓜ Rato

R de São Bento

R Artilharia 1

AV Duarte Pacheco

R das Amoreiras

R Dom João V

R do Sol ao Rato

For reviews see	
❶ Top Experiences	p120
❻ Sights	p124
❸ Eating	p125
❸ Drinking	p128
❸ Entertainment	p129
❸ Shopping	p129

Sights

Museu Calouste Gulbenkian – Coleção Moderna

MUSEUM

1 MAP P122, C2

Situated in a sculpture-dotted garden, the Coleção Moderna reveals a stellar collection of 20th-century Portuguese and international art. Admission includes the separately housed Coleção do Fundador. The Museu Calouste Gulbenkian – Coleção Moderna is currently closed for renovations (due to reopen in 2023). (Modern Collection; www.gulbenkian.pt)

Casa-Museu Medeiros e Almeida

MUSEUM

2 MAP P122, D7

Housed in a stunning early-19th-century mansion, this little-known museum presents António Medeiros e Almeida's exquisite fine- and decorative-arts collection. Highlights include Han ceramics and

Free Museum & Gallery Entry

Save museum and gallery visits for the weekend. The Museu Calouste Gulbenkian museums (Coleção do Fundador and Coleção Moderna) both offer free entry on Sunday after 2pm, while the Casa-Museu Medeiros e Almeida is free from 10am to 1pm on the first Saturday of the month.

Ming- and Qing-dynasty porcelain, Thomas Gainsborough paintings, a 300-strong stockpile of watches and clocks (one of the best private collections in Europe), and a dinner service that once belonged to Napoleon Bonaparte. (www.casa-museumedeirosealmeida.pt)

Mãe d'Água

HISTORIC BUILDING

3 MAP P122, B7

The king laid the Aqueduto das Águas Livres' final stone at Mãe d'Água, the city's massive 5500-cu-metre main reservoir. Completed in 1834, the reservoir's cool, echoing chamber is a fine place to admire 19th-century technology. Climb the stairs for a view of the aqueduct and the surrounding neighbourhood. Admission is €5 if there's an exhibition on. (Mother of Water; www.epal.pt/EPAL/menu/museu-da-água)

Parque Eduardo VII

PARK

4 MAP P122, C5

An urban oasis with British roots, Parque Eduardo VII is named after Edward VII, who visited Lisbon in 1903. The sloping parterre affords sweeping views over the whizzing traffic of Praça Marquês de Pombal to the river.

Estufas

GARDENS

5 MAP P122, B4

Tucked away in a pocket of Parque Eduardo VII, this trio of glasshouses nurtures tree ferns and camellias in the estufa fría

Mãe d'Água

(cool greenhouse), coffee and mango trees in the *estufa quente* (hot greenhouse) and cacti in the *estufa doce* (sweet greenhouse). (Greenhouses)

Jardim Botânico

GARDENS

6 ⊙ MAP P122, D8

Nurtured by green-fingered students, the Jardim Botânico is a quiet, 1500-species pocket of lushness tucked away from the bustling Jardim do Príncipe Real on a hill overlooking Lisbon's Baixa neighbourhood. Look out for Madeiran geraniums, sequoias, purple jacarandas and, by the entrance (upper-level gardens), a gigantic Moreton Bay fig tree. It's also worth a peek inside the butterfly house. (Botanical Garden; www.mnhnc.ulisboa.pt)

Eating

Tasca Fit

HEALTH FOOD €

7 ✕ MAP P122, F2

Spacious and brightly decorated, this restaurant serves affordable, healthy, sugar-free food, served in the generous portions that are often found in *tascas*. It's one of the few in the area serving vegetarian options (*feijoada*, a normally meat-heavy stew, and lentil burgers) and Brazilian-style tapioca offerings (a type of crêpe). (www.tascafit.pt)

Pastelaria Versailles

PASTRIES €

8 ✕ MAP P122, E2

With a marble chandelier and icing-sugar stucco confection, this sublime patisserie is where the smart set come to gossip and

Aqueduct of the Free Waters

The 109 arches of the **Aqueduto das Águas Livres** lope across the hills into Lisbon from Caneças, more than 18km away; they are most spectacular at Campolide, where the tallest arch is an incredible 65m high. Built between 1728 and 1835, by order of Dom João V, the aqueduct is a spectacular feat of engineering and brought Lisbon its first clean drinking water. Its more sinister claim to fame is as the site where 19th-century mass murderer Diogo Alves pushed his victims over the edge. No prizes for guessing why it was closed to the public soon after.

devour cream cakes (or scones with jam), espresso with *sortidos Húngaros* (chocolate-covered cookies) and house-spawned chocolate cake (served disc-shaped; it's oh, so decadent!).

Avenida SushiCafé   JAPANESE €€

9 MAP P122, D7

Don't let the flagship location of what is essentially a mall-food-court sushi chain fool you: Chef Daniel Rente creates some surprisingly and seriously good Japanese fusion here. (www.sushicafe.pt)

Forno d'Oro   PIZZA €€

10 MAP P122, C6

True to its name, Lisbon's most serious pizzeria indeed produces pies out of a golden (brick) oven. The burrata and buffalo mozzarella here is flown in daily from Italy, and pizzas feature PDO-protected ingredients from the motherland (parma ham, Culatello di Zibello

salami). Seasonal specials shake up the status quo, like San Marzano tomatoes, *fior di latte,* nettle pesto and acorn-fed *porco preto*. (www.fornodoro.pt)

Gourmet Experience   FOOD HALL €€

11 MAP P122, C3

The previously underused 7th floor of Lisbon's fanciest department store was transformed into the Gourmet Experience in late 2017. A supersized version of a gourmet food hall idea imported from Madrid, this high-end food court with table service is a culinary cornucopia of top Lisboan and Iberian chefs. (www.elcorteingles.pt/gourmet-experience)

Jesus é Goês   INDIAN €€

12 MAP P122, E8

At one of Lisbon's best Indian restaurants, jovial chef Jesus Lee whips up contemporary Goan delicacies. Rice-sack tablecloths and colourful murals (note the playful Christian-Hindu imagery) set the scene for starters such as onion-coriander chickpea fritters or potato bhaji with puri, followed by mushroom and chestnut or shrimp curries, or 11-spices goat – all fiery-fantastic. Reserve ahead – it's tiny. Cash only.

Cervejaria Ribadouro
SEAFOOD €€

13 MAP P122, E7

Bright, noisy and full to the gills, this bustling beer hall is popular with local seafood fans, some of whom just belly up to the bar, chase their fresh shrimp and *tremoços* (lupin beans) with an ice-cold *imperial* (draught beer) and call it a night. The shellfish are plucked fresh from the tank, weighed and cooked to lip-smacking perfection. (www.cervejariaribadouro.pt)

Zaafran
INDIAN €€

14 MAP P122, F3

Mozambican-raised Indians run this subcontinental gem near Saldanha, an affordable option in the area and an alternative to the nearby shopping centre's food courts. The lunch *thalis* (platters) are authentic (from €9.90), the accompanying salsas are legit hot, and Mozambican influences, especially in the prawn dishes and specials like peanut curries, shake things up enough that the menu is nontraditional Indian.

Os Tibetanos
VEGETARIAN €€

15 MAP P122, D7

Lisbon's oldest herbivore temple is part of a Tibetan Buddhism school. Its mantra is fresh vegetarian food, with daily specials such as quiche and curry. Sit in the serene courtyard if the sun's out and save room for the rose-petal ice cream. (www.tibetanos.com)

Horta dos Brunos
PORTUGUESE €€€

16 MAP P122, F3

Chef Pedro Filipe's somewhat unknown and unassuming gourmet *tasca*, a favourite among moving and shaking politicians and in-the-know gastronauts, does some of Lisbon's best work. There's a menu, but stick to your server's rundown of what's cooking daily, such as extraordinary tuna, cuttlefish *à lagareiro* (baked in a sea of fragrant olive oil) and succulent

Exploring the Avenida

The tree-fringed 19th-century Avenida da Liberdade is a 1.1km-long ribbon of style, linking Praça dos Restauradores in the south to the busy Marquês de Pombal roundabout in the north. This is Lisbon's classic strolling boulevard, flanked by some of the city's choicest hotels, cafes and designer boutiques.

lamb chops, all beautifully presented and modern in execution. There are top-end French wines, too.

Drinking

Red Frog COCKTAIL BAR

17 🚇 MAP P122, E7

In true speakeasy fashion, Red Frog is accessed via a 'Press for Cocktails' doorbell and a list of rules. Enter a sophisticated mixology world of craft cocktails and appropriate glassware, dress and behaviour. (www.facebook.com/redfrogspeakeasy)

Sky Bar BAR

18 🚇 MAP P122, D7

Wow, what a view! This high-rise bar at the Tivoli has a gorgeous terrace, full of minimalist white nooks for sipping expensive cocktails (€12 to €17), conversing and drinking in the panorama of Lisbon. (www.skybarrooftop.com)

JNcQUOI Delibar COCKTAIL BAR

19 🚇 MAP P122, E7

A lavish bar fit for its chic address, this ground-level drinking den below the upscale restaurant of the same name caters to a well-heeled crowd who gather around the long, contorted marble bar – the centrepiece of a top-end deli slinging gourmet provisions – to chase cold bar delicacies (fresh oysters, caviar) with exquisite spirits. (www.jncquoi.com)

El Corte Inglés

Entertainment

Fundação Calouste Gulbenkian
CLASSICAL MUSIC

20 ⭐ MAP P122, B1

Home to the Gulbenkian Orchestra, this classical-music heavyweight stages first-rate concerts and ballets. (www.gulbenkian.pt)

Shopping

Carbono
MUSIC

21 🔒 MAP P122, F7

The staff may be grumpy here, but it's hard not to like Carbono, with its impressive selection of new and second-hand vinyl and CDs. World music – West African boogaloo, Brazilian tropicalia – is especially well represented. (www.carbono.com.pt)

Leya Buchholz
BOOKS

22 🔒 MAP P122, D6

Leya Buchholz has a sizeable collection of literature in Portuguese and English, plus in-store readings. (www.leya.com)

One-Roof Shopping

Lisboêtas with a hankering for luxury goods, gourmet food and imported fashion and design head straight to Spanish department store **El Corte Inglés** (Map p122, C3; www.elcorteingles.pt), a nine-floor extravaganza of 800-thread-count linens, truffled chocolates, Swarovski crystal and all things luxurious in between. The city's top supermarket is here, too – a gourmand lifeblood for trendy locals and expats alike.

Luis Onofre
SHOES

23 🔒 MAP P122, D6

For sexy women's shoes (from €308) fit for a princess, it doesn't get any bigger than Portugal's Luis Onofre, who has even been known to bedazzle high heels with Swarovski crystal! Michelle Obama, Naomi Watts and Paris Hilton are among Onofre's fans. (www.luisonofre.com)

Estrela, Lapa & Alcântara

In quiet, tree-lined Estrela and Lapa you can easily tiptoe off the well-trodden trail along cafe-rimmed squares, lanes with breezy river views, and gentrified streets where 18th-century mansions harbour antique stores, boutiques and galleries. Down by the river, Alcântara signals a new age for Lisbon: its once-industrial warehouses have been reborn as en-vogue bars, clubs and restaurants.

The Short List

○ **Basílica da Estrela (p136)** *Marvelling at this 1790 neoclassical basilica, including the stunning nativity scene and expansive rooftop views over Lisbon.*

○ **Museu da Marioneta (p136)** *Discovering your inner child at this enchanting puppet museum.*

○ **Museu Nacional de Arte Antiga (p132)** *Wandering the hallowed halls in this world-class museum set inside a 17th-century palace.*

○ **Museu do Oriente (p136)** *Admiring priceless Asian antiquities in this museum occupying a revamped 1940s bacalhau (dried salt-cod) warehouse.*

Getting There & Around

🚋 Tram 15E from Praça da Figueira and tram 18E from Cais do Sodré go to Santos and Alcântara. Tram 25 trundles to Santos, Lapa and Estrela. Tram 28 is also convenient for Estrela.

🚌 Buses 713 (Arco do Cego–Estação Campolide) and 727 (Estação Roma–Areeiro–Restelo) stop in Estrela, Lapa and Alcântara. Bus 712 is useful for Alcântara.

Estrela, Lapa & Alcântara Map on p134

Top Experience 📷
Discover Art & Relics at Museu Nacional de Arte Antiga

On its scenic perch above the river, this 17th-century palace is a grand backdrop for Lisbon's foremost ancient-art collection. Meissen porcelain, Portuguese sculpture, Beauvais tapestry, Ming porcelain, baroque silverware and Japanese screens do a stellar job of whisking you through the world of fine and decorative arts from the Middle Ages to the 19th century.

◉ MAP P134, E4

National Museum of Ancient Art

www.museudearteantiga.pt

Panels of St Vincent

Covering an entire wall (room 2; 3rd floor), the *Panels of St Vincent* are the museum's pride and joy. Attributed to Nuno Gonçalves, the painter of Dom Afonso V, and dating to 1470, the expressive polyptych depicts the veneration of St Vincent.

Monstrance & Cross

The gold and silverware collection's two standouts hide in room 29. Gil Vicente's golden wonder, the Monstrance of Belém (1506), is made from the gold brought back from Vasco da Gama's second voyage to India, and embellished with armillary spheres and the 12 Apostles. Just as dazzling is the 1214 processional cross of Dom Sancho I, delicately engraved and bejewelled with pearls and sapphires.

European Painting

Strong on ecclesiastical painting, this collection takes a blockbuster tour of 14th- to 19th-century European art. Two pieces in particular stand out. The first is a Renaissance masterpiece, Albrecht Dürer's chiaroscuro *St Jerome* (1521). The second is Hieronymus Bosch's devotional triptych, *St Anthony* (1500), an evocative depiction of the hermit being attacked by demons and faced with sins like gluttony and abandonment of the faith.

Oriental Art & Ceramics

Exquisite 16th-century Indian caskets inlaid with mother of pearl, Ming porcelain and geometric tiles from Syria and Turkey all beg exploration on the 2nd floor. Be sure to see the beautifully gilded Namban screens, depicting the arrival of the Namban (southern barbarians), the Portuguese navigators who arrived in Japan in 1543.

★ Top Tips

○ This museum is simply huge, so pick up a map at the entrance to pinpoint what you really want to see. Allow a minimum of two hours.

○ Arrive early or late to dodge the crowds.

○ Biannual temporary themed exhibitions (priced separately, at around €6) are reached via a second entrance on Rua das Janelas Verdes.

✕ Take a Break

Step next door to Le Chat (p140) for drinks and snacks on the terrace with captivating river views.

Quimera Brewpub (p140), 800m west, does craft beer and cocktails inside a cinematic, stone-walled 18th-century carriage tunnel.

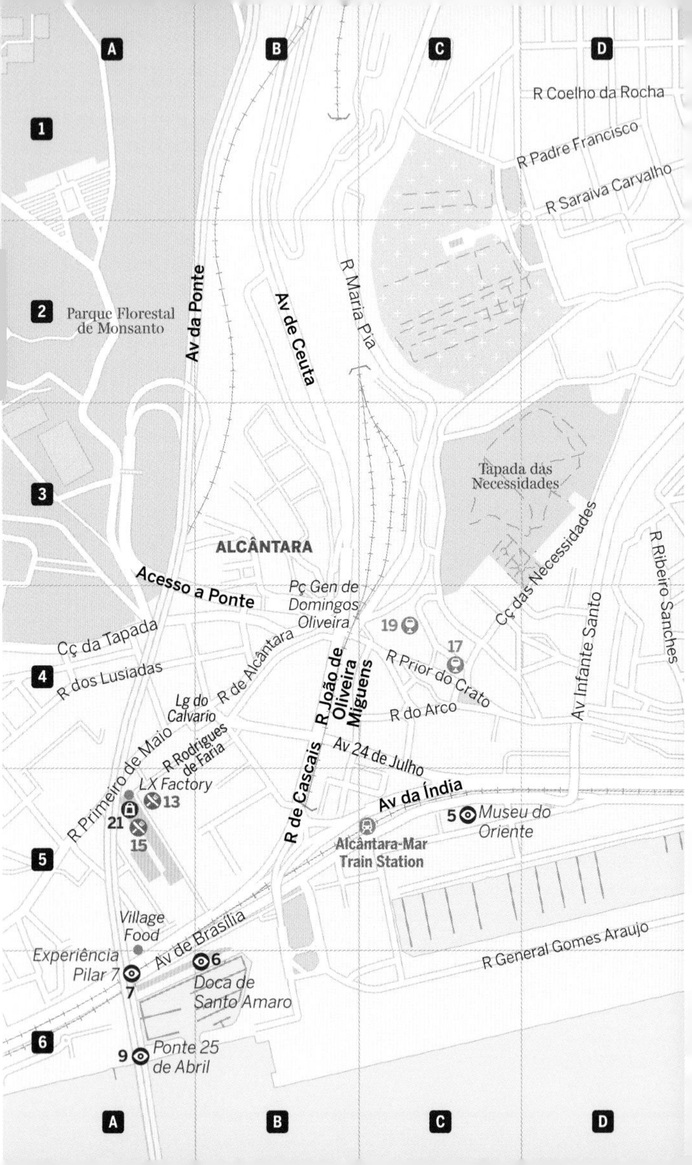

A

B

C

D

1

R Coelho da Rocha

R Padre Francisco

R Saraiva Carvalho

2 Parque Florestal de Monsanto

Av da Ponte

Av de Ceuta

R Maria Pia

3

Tapada das Necessidades

ALCÂNTARA

Acesso a Ponte

Pç Gen de Domingos Oliveira

Cç das Necessidades

R Ribeiro Sanches

Cç da Tapada

4 R dos Lusiadas

R de Alcântara

R João de Oliveira Miguens

19 🚇

R Prior do Crato

17 🚇

R do Arco

Av Infante Santo

Lg do Calvario

R Rodrigues de Faria

Av 24 de Julho

R de Cascais

LX Factory

21 🔒 ⊗ 13

⊗

5 15

Av da Índia

5 ⊙ Museu do Oriente

Alcântara-Mar Train Station

Village Food

Experiência Pilar 7

Av de Brasília

⊙ 6

6 7

Doca de Santo Amaro

R General Gomes Araujo

9 ⊙ Ponte 25 de Abril

A

B

C

D

E **8** Casa Fernando Pessoa

R de São Jorge

R do Patrocínio

Casa Museu de Amália Rodrigues **4**

Jardim da Estrela **2**

Pç da Estrela

R de Santo Amaro

R dos Prazeres

R de São Bento

16 Tv Santa Teresa

R de São Marçal

R de São Jasmim

R do Jasmim

R Academia Ciências

Lg de Jesus

Basílica da Estrela **1**

ESTRELA

R de São Bernardo

R da Imprensa

Cç da Estrela

14

R dos Navegantes

R da Bela Vista à Lapa

R de Borges Caneiro

Av Infante Santo

R de Sant'ana à Lapa

R de São Domingos à Lapa

R da Lapa

R do Meio à Lapa

20

R do Quelhas

R das Trinas

12

R das Praças

R dos Remédios

MADRAGOA

R do Sacremento a Lapa

R das Janelas Verdes

LAPA

R Garcia da Horta

R do Conde

R do Pau de Bandeira

Museu da Marioneta **3**

11

R da Esperança

Cç Marquês de Abrantes

Lg de Santos

R de Santos-o-Velho

Cç Ribeiro Santos

R dos Polais de São Bento

R dos Poço dos Negros

Lg do Conde Barão **22**

R da Silva

Av Dom Carlos 1

R Dom Luis 1

R da Boavista

Av 24 de Julho

Santos Train Station

Cais da Viscondessa

23 R do Olival

R Presidente Arriaga

18 Museu Nacional de Arte Antiga

Av 24 de Julho

Av de Brasília

Doca de Alcântara

10

Rio Tejo

For reviews see	
⊙ Top Experiences	p132
⊙ Sights	p136
⊗ Eating	p138
🍷 Drinking	p139
✿ Entertainment	p141
🔒 Shopping	p141

N

0 — 500 m
0 — 0.25 miles

Sights

Basílica da Estrela   CHURCH

1 MAP P134, F2

The curvaceous, sugar-white dome and twin belfries of Basílica da Estrela are visible from afar. The echoing interior is awash with pink-and-black marble, which creates a kaleidoscopic effect when you gaze up into the cupola. The neoclassical beauty was completed in 1790 by order of Dona Maria I (whose tomb is here) in gratitude for a male heir.

Jardim da Estrela   GARDENS

2 MAP P134, F1

Seeking green respite? Opposite the Basílica da Estrela, this 1852 green space is perfect for a stroll, with paths weaving past pine, monkey-puzzle and palm trees, rose and cacti beds, and the centrepiece – a giant banyan tree. Kids love the duck ponds and animal-themed playground. There

are several open-air cafes where you can recharge.

Museu da Marioneta   MUSEUM

3 MAP P134, G3

Discover your inner child at the surprisingly enchanting Museu da Marioneta, a veritable Geppetto's workshop housed in the 17th-century Convento das Bernardas. Alongside superstars such as impish Punch and his Portuguese equivalent Dom Roberto are rarities: Vietnamese water puppets, Sicilian opera marionettes and intricate Burmese shadow puppets. Check out the fascinating exhibit of the making of the animation film *A Suspeita*. (Puppet Museum; www. museudamarioneta.pt)

Casa Museu de Amália Rodrigues   MUSEUM

4 MAP P134, G1

A pilgrimage site for fado fans, this is where the Rainha do Fado (Queen of Fado) Amália Rodrigues (1920-99) lived; note the *calçada portuguesa* (Portuguese sidewalk design) announcing 'Amália'. Short tours take in portraits, glittering costumes and crackly recordings of her performances. Reservations are recommended. (www.amaliarodrigues.pt)

Museu do Oriente   MUSEUM

5 MAP P134, C5

The beautifully designed Museu do Oriente highlights Portugal's ties with Asia, from its first steps

---

Waterfront Walkabout

One of Lisbon's best and most atmospheric spots for a stroll stretches from Torre de Belém to Doca de Santo Amaro (and beyond) – a leisurely 4km promenade hugging the Rio Tejo. Join *lisboêtas* with a cocktail or an ice cream and lap up the local colour along this festive esplanade.

in Macau to ancestor worship. The cavernous museum occupies a revamped 1940s *bacalhau* (dried salt-cod) warehouse – a €30-million conversion. Strikingly displayed in pitch-black rooms, the permanent collection focuses on the Portuguese presence in Asia, and Asian gods. (www.museudo oriente.pt)

Doca de Santo Amaro
LANDMARK

6 ◉ MAP P134, B6

This group of old warehouses have been converted into a lovely patch of restaurants and bars, all with stupendous views over the marina and Ponte 25 de Abril.

Experiência Pilar 7
VIEWPOINT

7 ◉ MAP P134, A6

Experiência Pilar 7 affords the opportunity to get up close and personal with the iconic Ponte 25 de Abril (p138) from 80m above ground. The €5.3-million attraction, opened in late 2017, includes a walk-through multimedia tour of the Golden Gate–lookalike bridge that's a real treat for engineering buffs, particularly the (vertigo-inducing) transition between the suspended metal bridge and the concrete viaduct, and the fascinating twin rooms where the main moorings of the support cables are visible. Kids will also be impressed. (www.visitlisboa.com)

Jardim da Estrela

Double-Decker Dining

An offshoot of what was originally a London cultural project, Village Underground Lisboa is hidden inside the Carris complex in Alcântara. The multiuse space houses the fun **Village Food** (Map p134, A5; www.vulisboa. com), located inside a raised antique double-decker city bus resting on shipping containers (great for kids). Most tourists don't wander in here, despite it being visible from Avenida Brasília and Ponte 25 de Abril.

Casa Fernando Pessoa
CULTURAL CENTRE

8 MAP P134, E1

Immerse yourself in the life and work of Portuguese modernist founder and author Fernando Pessoa as you wander through his old apartment, browse his book collection (digitised), attempt to decipher some of his handwritten notes, and admire paintings of the author by fellow members of the movement, such as painter Júlio Pomar. (www. casafernandopessoa.pt)

Ponte 25 de Abril
BRIDGE

9 MAP P134, A6

Most people experience visual déjà vu the first time they clap eyes on the bombastic suspension bridge Ponte 25 de Abril. It's hardly surprising given that it's the spitting image of San Francisco's Golden Gate Bridge, was constructed by the same company in 1966 and, at 2.27km, is almost as long. (www. lusoponte.pt)

Eating

Último Porto
SEAFOOD €€

10 MAP P134, E5

An absolute local's secret for a reason, this top seafooder takes an act of God to find. Hidden among the shipping-container cranes of the Port of Lisbon, its fantastically simple grilled fish paired with top Alentejan and Douro wines draws locals in droves. Framed by containers and departmental port buildings, the staff oversees a car-park-style grill.

Petiscaria Ideal
FUSION €€

11 MAP P134, G3

This small, buzzing spot serves delicious *petiscos* (goat's cheese and honey toast, pork stew with pepper compote, *alheira* sausage-stuffed portobello mushrooms) followed by sweets like *medronho*-spiked chocolate mousse or pear crumble. The walls are clad with mismatching *azulejos*, dining is at long communal tables, and there's a spirited rock 'n' roll vibe to the place. (www. facebook.com/petiscariaideal/)

Clube de Jornalistas
PORTUGUESE €€

12 MAP P134, F3

You have to be determined to find hilltop Clube de Jornalistas, but persevere. This 18th-century house, opening onto a tree-shaded courtyard, has oodles of charm and serves Mediterranean and Portuguese dishes such as creamy Brazilian-style shrimp-stew risotto and black pork. The service is faultless, the food a worthy runner-up. (www.restauranteclubedejornalistas.com)

Cantina Lx CAFE €€

13 MAP P134, A5

Decked out like an industrial-chic country barn, this cool cafe in LX Factory is a laid-back pick for snacks, mains such as codfish and sirloin steak, and Sunday buffet. (www.cantinalx.com)

Loco PORTUGUESE €€€

14 MAP P134, F2

In the shadow of the Basílica da Estrela (p136), this fine-dining spot comes courtesy of chef Alexandre Silva, whose bold and modern take on Portuguese cuisine taps both tradition and travel on its way to a personality-rich gastronomic adventure. It offers a daily-changing, description-free tasting menu (you choose 18 'moments' with or without wine pairing), each steeped in sustainability and seasonality. (www.loco.pt)

1300 Taberna PORTUGUESE €€€

15 MAP P134, A5

A hodgepodge mess of rustic-chic chandeliers and exposed air ducts hovers over large communal-table seating at this LX Factory favourite. It dishes out creative and fun takes on Portuguese fare, many from its wood-fired grill, and is one of the best places in LX Factory for a drink. (www.1300taberna.com)

Drinking

Foxtrot BAR

16 MAP P134, H1

A cuckoo-clock doorbell announces new arrivals to this dark, decadent sliver of art-nouveau

Dine Like a Local

Senhor Uva At Senhor Uva, and its brother Senhor Manuel, just across the street, you can find organic food and a masterful natural wine list.

Sofia's Place Ana Sofia wants Sofia's Place to be an open house for people from all backgrounds to cook, share, dance, and express themselves. Good Creole food.

O Mercado Set inside the Alcântara market, this classic Portuguese restaurant is ideal for those looking for fresh fish and seafood, such as cockles *à bulhão pato*, grouper and prawn rice, or deep-fried sardines with tomato rice.

 Recommended by Inês Matos Andrade, *food writer and editor* @inesmatosandrade

glamour, in the bar business since 1978. Foxtrot keeps the mood mellow with jazzy beats and intensely attentive mixology detailed on a tracing-paper menu (cocktails €7 to €15). It's a wonderfully atmospheric spot for a drink. (www.barfoxtrot.pt)

Quimera Brewpub BREWERY

17 🚇 MAP P134, C4

An American-Brazilian couple launched Lisbon's second brewpub in 2016 with 12 beers, including rarer choices such as Belgian blonde ale, American dark lager and experimental brews, along with a few taps devoted to invited *lisboêta* suds from Dois Corvos, 8ª Colina, Lince and more. Downing proper pints within the Palácio das Necessidades' stone-

walled 18th-century carriage tunnel feels vaguely medieval. (www.quimerabrewpub.com)

Le Chat BAR

18 🚇 MAP P134, E4

Staring at the view of the docks and Ponte 25 de Abril (and construction cranes!) is the prime activity on the terrace of this glass-walled cafe-bar. It's a casual spot for coffee by day or cocktails (€9 to €15) and mellow beats by night. (www.lechat.pt)

Go A Lisboa ROOFTOP BAR

19 🚇 MAP P134, C4

A cocktail bar, restaurant and yoga studio merged into one. The owners took over the previously underused terrace of Casa de Goa

View of Ponte 25 de Abril (p138) from LX Factory

LUÍS OVERLANDER/SHUTTERSTOCK ©

and turned it into a green oasis complete with string lights and a view of the 25 de Abril bridge. The Goan roots remain on the menu, which features meaty samosas, curries and cardamom-infused gin and tonics. (www.goalisboa.com)

Entertainment

Senhor Vinho
LIVE MUSIC

20 ⭐ MAP P134, F3

Fado star Maria da Fé owns this small place, welcoming first-rate *fadistas* (fado singers). Go for the fado, not the food, and feel free to refuse menu extras. (www.srvinho.com)

Shopping

LX Market
MARKET

21 🔒 MAP P134, A5

Vintage clothing, antiques, crafts, food, and weird and wonderful plants – the LX Factory market is the place to find them. Live music keeps the Sunday shoppers entertained. (www.lxmarket.com.pt)

Comida Independente
FOOD & DRINKS

22 🔒 MAP P134, H3

This sustainably focused market has a lot going for it: free-range, preservative-free charcuterie from the Algarve, Vinhais and elsewhere; a 160-strong wine inventory, 80% of which are natural; organic *medronho* (Portuguese fruit brandy); gourmet *Pudim abade de*

LX Factory

Tune into Lisbon's creative pulse at **LX Factory** (Map p134, A5; www.lxfactory.com), housed in a cavernous 19th-century industrial complex. Abandoned warehouses have been transformed into spaces for art studios, galleries, workshops, and printing and design companies. There's a rustically cool cafe as well as a bookshop, several restaurants, design-minded shops and cultural spaces. Throughout the month, you'll find a dynamic menu of events, from live concerts and film screenings to fashion shows and art exhibitions. Weekend nights see parties with a dance- and art-loving crowd.

Priscos from Braga (a decadent flan swarming with egg yolk, sugar, 20-year-old port and cured ham); and top-notch cheese plates (€15 for one person, €25 for two). (www.comidaindependente.pt)

Portugal Gifts
GIFTS & SOUVENIRS

23 🔒 MAP P134, E4

This craft shop puts a contemporary spin on Portuguese souvenirs, with everything from Barcelos cockerel mugs to *azulejo* coasters and chocolate sardines. (www.facebook.com/portugalgifts)

Worth a Trip 🔭
Explore Sintra's Grand Palaces & Mystical Gardens

Settle amid a lush forest lies the charming Unesco-listed town of Sintra. The two sugary white conical chimneys of Palácio Nacional de Sintra rise above the green to welcome those approaching the village. Quinta da Regaleira (pictured), with its mystical gardens, is also a sight to behold, while the Palácio Biester, renovated in 2022, is a romantic gem yet to be explored.

Getting There

Catch a train here from Rossio (€2.30, 40 minutes) and Oriente (€2.30, 50 minutes) stations.

Royal Taste

Take in arabesque courtyards, barley-twist columns and 15th- and 16th-century geometric *azulejos* (hand-painted tiles) as you wander through the Palácio Nacional de Sintra. Don't miss the Sala dos Cisnes with its frescos of 27 gold-collared *cisnes* (swans), the Sala dos Brasões adorned with blue-and-white tile panels depicting hunting scenes, and swing by the large kitchen to see where the royals cooked their banquet feasts.

Picture Setting

Before opening its doors to visitors, Palácio de Biester made its film debut in Roman Polanski's *Ninth Gate*. Strolling through the gardens gives you a chance to see Sintra from afar. From its two viewpoints, you can spot all the major historical sights and truly appreciate the beauty of Europe's first Unesco Cultural Landscape.

Mystical Gardens

Among Quinta da Regaleira's mystical sites is an 88ft-deep well. The Poço Iniciático, as it is known, is thought to have been used for Masonic initiation rituals. A spiral staircase leads you to the bottom passing through nine landings which may represent the 'nine circles of hell' and the 'nine circles of purgatory'. As you look down, you'll spot a compass rose topped with a Templar cross. The chase for symbols continues through the gardens' numerous grottoes and lakes.

★ Getting around Sintra

○ Arrive early or late to avoid the biggest crowds.

○ Buy a Parques de Sintra Monte da Lua combo ticket, which saves 5% to 10% on admission depending on how many sites you choose.

○ Pena Palace and Sintra's Moorish castle are on the outskirts of town. It's quite a trek uphill (1 hour at least). Save your energy by jumping on bus 434 or hailing a taxi or a tuk-tuk.

✗ Take a Break

Since 1756, **Fábrica das Verdadeiras Queijadas da Sapa** (www.facebook.com/queijadasdasapa) has been rotting royal teeth with *queijadas*, pastry shells filled with a marzipan-like mix of fresh cheese, sugar, flour and cinnamon.

Casa Piriquita (www.piriquita.pt) tempts with the luscious *travesseiro* (puff pastry filled with almond-and-egg-yolk cream).

Survival Guide

Gare do Oriente (p115) ARCHITECT: SANTIAGO CALATRAVA. ZOIA KOSTINA/SHUTTERSTOCK ©

Before You Go

Book Your Stay

o Book ahead during high season (mid-July to mid-September).

o Many guesthouses lack lifts, meaning you'll have to haul your luggage up three flights or more. If this disconcerts, be sure to book a place with a lift.

o *Pensões* and *residenciais* are small-scale guesthouses, often with a personal feel. The best are generally better than the cheapest hotels. Rates usually include breakfast.

o Hotels normally drop prices in low season.

o Short-stay apartments are an alternative to hotels.

Useful Websites

Lisbon Lux (www.lisbonlux.com) Hip local guide to all things Lisbon, including accommodation.

Go Lisbon (www.golis bon.com) Local guide

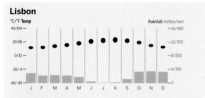

Lisbon

When to Go

o **Winter** (Nov–Feb) Quiet except for Carnival in February. Low-season deals available. Weather can be wet and windy.

o **Spring** (Mar–May) Parks in bloom, mild and often sunny days, accommodation still reasonably priced – perfect season for exploring.

o **Summer** (Jun–Aug) Usually hot. Best time for open-air festivals, beach days and alfresco dining. Rooms are at a premium; book ahead.

o **Autumn** (Sep–Oct) Pleasant temps, culture-focused events and few crowds, though showers are to be expected.

with hotels, apartments, hostels and *pousadas* (upmarket inns), divided by various categories of interest.

Lonely Planet (www.lonelyplanet.com/portugal/lisbon/hotels) Recommendations and bookings.

Best Budget

Lisbon Calling (www.lisboncalling.net) A lovely Santa Catarina backpackers hostel with original frescos,

azulejos and hardwood floors.

Lisbon Destination Hostel (www.desti nationhostels.com) World-class hostel housed in Lisbon's loveliest train station.

Home Lisbon Hostel (www.homelisbonhos tel.com) Family-run hostel in the heart of Baixa with top-end facilities, including an atmospheric bar.

Independente (www.theindependente.pt)

Stylish boutique option across from the dramatic Miradouro de São Pedro de Alcântara.

Living Lounge (www.livingloungehostel.com) Straddling Chiado and Baixa, and steeped in vintage cool, this social hostel oozes restrained hipness.

Best Midrange

Casa do Príncipe (www.casadoprincipe.com) Excellent-value nine-room B&B occupying a 19th-century neo-Moorish palace.

Lisbon Story Guesthouse (www.lisbonstoryguesthouse.com) Wonderful guesthouse with themed rooms overlooking lively Largo de São Domingos.

Casa Amora (www.casaamora.com) Discerning and stylish boutique hotel with lovely gardens and personalised service near historic Mãe d'Àgua.

Dear Lisbon (www.dearlisbon.com) Tasteful art-decorated rooms with a chilled courtyard pool.

Casa de São Mamede (www.casadesaomamede.pt) Near the botanical gardens, this 18th-century, family-run villa has rooms set with period furnishings.

Best Top End

Palacete Chafariz d'el Rei (www.chafarizdelrei.com) Boutique, six-suite 20th-century mansion in Alfama.

Santiago de Alfama (www.santiagodealfama.com) A ruined 15th-century palace turned boutique gem in Alfama.

Valverde (www.valverdehotel.com) Exquisitely curated, high-design 25-room boutique hotel inside a luxury converted townhouse on Avenida da Liberdade.

Memmo Alfama (www.memmoalfama.com) Trendy boutique hotel with stunning views over Alfama from its roof terrace.

Pestana Palace Lisboa (www.pestana.com/pt/hotel/pestana-palace) Italian architect Nicola Bigaglia's 1904 Valle Flor Palace – a National Monument – houses this historically stunning hotel.

Arriving in Lisbon

Aeroporto de Lisboa

o Around 6km north of the centre, the ultra-modern Aeroporto de Lisboa operates direct flights to major international hubs.

o The airport is connected to central Lisbon by metro (a single costs €1.50). It is the terminus of the red line.

o A taxi into central Lisbon should cost around €16, plus €1.60 for luggage. Avoid queues by flagging one down at the Departures hall.

o Unlike taxis, ride-sharing services such as Uber and Bolt can only do pickups outside the Departures zone on the 2nd floor. At Arrivals, take the escalator to your right.

Estação Santa Apolónia

o Metro services run every few minutes, providing speedy connections to central Lisbon. A

Tickets & Passes

There are two useful cards for catching public transport around the city; both can be purchased from kiosks in the metro stations.

o Navegante costs €0.50, to which you can then add credit in various denominations. Select the 'zapping' option, rather than a single trip (only valid for the metro), which allows the card to be used on the metro, buses, trams and funiculars. Pay-as-you go fares are €1.35 on metro and Carris (buses and trams).

o A 24-hour Carris/metro pass costs €6.45 and allows unlimited travel over a 24-hour period on all buses, trams, funiculars and the metro.

o Validate your ticket at the station entrance.

o Useful signs include 'correspondência' (transfer between lines) and 'saída' (exit to the street).

Tram, Bus & Funicular

o Carris (www.carris.pt) operates buses, trams and funiculars.

o Buses and trams run from about 5am or 6am to 1am; there are some night bus and tram services.

o Pick up a transport map from tourist offices or Carris kiosks, which are dotted around the city. The Carris website has timetables and route details.

o Individual tickets cost €2 on buses, €3 on trams; they can be purchased on board. Buy 24-hour Carris passes (€6.45) from ticket machines or kiosks at metro stations.

o A return funicular journey costs €3.80, except the Elevador de Santa Justa, which costs €5.30.

o Always validate your ticket.

single ticket costs €1.50 to anywhere in the city.

o Santa Apolónia is on the blue line, one stop from Terreiro do Paço (Praça do Comércio), the heart of downtown Lisbon.

Gare do Oriente

o The ultramodern Gare do Oriente is on the red metro line, which provides quick and frequent connections to central Lisbon.

o Baixa-Chiado in central Lisbon is a 20-minute metro ride away. Change for the green line at Alameda.

o Bus services linking Gare do Oriente to central Lisbon include

the 708 to Martim Moniz (via the airport). Single tickets cost €2 on board (€1.50 pre-paid).

Getting Around

Metro

o Compact and easy to navigate, the Lisbon Metro (www.metrolisboa.pt) has just four lines: red, green, yellow and blue.

o The metro runs from 6.30am to 1am.

o Buy tickets from the machines at metro stations; a single costs €1.50.

Bicycle

∘ Traffic, trams, hills and cobbles make cycling a challenging prospect. There are pleasant rides along a bike lane beside the Rio Tejo, however.

∘ A handy place to rent bikes is **Bike Iberia** (www.bikeiberia.com), a short stroll from Cais do Sodré.

∘ For shorter trips, you can use **Gira** (www.gira-bicicletasdelisboa.pt), the city's bike-sharing scheme with 48 stations around the city (and more on the way).

Taxi & Ride-Share

∘ Taxis in Lisbon are plentiful. Try the ranks at Rossio and Praça dos Restauradores, near stations and ferry terminals.

∘ The fare on the meter should read €3.25 (day-time minimum fare).

∘ You will be charged extra for luggage and 20% more for journeys from 9pm to 6am.

∘ Many locals prefer to use taxi apps and ride-share services, which are markedly cheaper than conventional taxis. A few popular apps include Uber (www.uber. com), Bolt (www.bolt.eu) and Taxi-Link (www.taxi-link.com).

Essential Information

Accessible Travel

Lisbon's airport is wheelchair accessible. Newer hotels tend to have some adapted rooms, though the facilities may not be up to scratch; some hostels have facilities for people with disabilities.

Lisbon, with its cobbled streets and hills, may be difficult for travellers with disabilities, but not impossible. Baixa's flat grid and Belém are fine, and all the sights at Parque das Nações are accessible.

Download Lonely Planet's free Accessible Travel guides from https://shop.lonelyplanet.com/categories/accessible-travel.com.

Accessible Portugal (www.accessibleportugal.com) This Portuguese association promotes accessible tourism and is the brains behind the **TUR4all Portugal** website, which works like a database of accessible tourist resources and services throughout Portugal and Spain.

Business Hours

Many shops close on Sundays and some shut early on Saturdays; small boutiques may also close for lunch (1pm to 3pm). Many museums are closed on Mondays.

Restaurants noon to 3pm and 7pm to 10pm

Cafes 8am to midnight

Shops 9.30am to 7pm Monday to Friday, to 1pm Saturday

Bars 7pm to 3am

Nightclubs 11pm to 6am Thursday to Saturday

Banks 8.30am to 3pm Monday to Friday

Discount Cards

The **Lisboa Card** offers unlimited use of public transport (including trains to Sintra and Cascais), entry to all key museums and attractions, and discounts of up to 50% on tours, cruises and other

Money-Saving Tips

o If you're on a budget, save your sightseeing for Sunday mornings, when entry to the majority of Lisbon's museums is free.

o Most sights have concessions (up to 50%) for youths, students and seniors – make sure you bring appropriate ID.

o Lisbon's top sights and attractions usually offer free entry for children under 12 (occasionally under 14).

admission charges. It's available at **Ask Me Lisboa tourist offices** (www.visitlisboa.com), including the one at the airport. The 24-/48-/72-hour versions cost €21/35/44. Validate the card when you want to start using it.

Electricity

Type C
220V/50Hz

Type F
230V/50Hz

Emergencies

Police, Fire & Ambulance (📞112)

Money

Currency

The Portuguese currency is the euro (€), divided into 100 cents.

ATMs

ATMs (Multibancos) are the easiest way to access your money. You just need your card and PIN. Your home bank will usually charge around 1.5% per transaction.

Credit Cards

Visa is widely accepted, as is MasterCard; American Express and Diners Club less so, with the exception of top-end hotels and restaurants.

Tipping

Service is not usually added to the bill. In touristy areas, 10% is fine, though it's never expected (few Portuguese ever leave more than a round-up to the nearest euro).

Public Holidays

Banks, offices, department stores and some shops close on public holidays.

New Year's Day 1 January

Carnaval Tuesday February/March – the day before Ash Wednesday

Good Friday March/April

Liberty Day 25 April – celebrating the 1974 revolution

Labour Day 1 May

Corpus Christi May/June – ninth Thursday after Easter

Portugal Day 10 June – also known as Camões and Communities Day

St Anthony's Day 13 June

Feast of the Assumption 15 August

Republic Day 5 October – commemorating the 1910 declaration of the Portuguese Republic

All Saints' Day 1 November

Independence Day 1 December – commemorating the 1640 restoration of independence from Spain

Feast of the Immaculate Conception 8 December

Christmas Day 25 December

Safe Travel

Lisbon generally enjoys a low crime rate, but petty theft is on the rise.

o Mind your wallet on trams – major hotspots for pickpockets – and other tourist hubs such as Rua Augusta.

o Pay attention at night around Anjos, Martim Moniz and Intendente metro stations, where muggings have occurred. Take care in dark alleys around Alfama and Graça.

o Always keep your wits about you in Cais do Sodré, which has seen an increase in snatch-and-grabs.

Toilets

Public toilets in Lisbon are rare. Train, metro and bus stations generally have public conveniences. Your best bet is to pop into the nearest cafe or bar. If you just want to use the loo, order a *bica* (espresso) – one of the cheapest things on the menu.

Dos & Don'ts

Greetings When greeting females or mixed company, an air kiss on both cheeks is common courtesy. Men give each other a handshake.

'Free' appetisers Whatever you eat, you must pay for, whether or not you ordered it.

It's common practice for restaurants to bring bread, butter, cheese and other goodies to the table – it's *not* a scam! – but these are *never free* and will be added to your bill at the end. If you don't want them, a polite 'no, thank you' will see them returned to the kitchen.

Language This is not Spain – speaking Spanish in Portugal won't win you any favours.

Tourist Information

Central Offices

Ask Me Lisboa (www.visitlisboa.com) provides tourist info, left luggage and charged internet access. There are branches in Praça dos Restauradores and Praça do Comércio.

Information Kiosks

Information kiosks (www.visitlisboa.com) can be found in these locations:

o Aeroporto de Lisboa

o Mosteiro dos Jerónimos

o Belém Tower

o Cais do Sodré

Language

Most sounds in Portuguese are also found in English. The exceptions are the nasal vowels (represented in our pronunciation guides by '*ng*' after the vowel), pronounced as if you're trying to make the sound through your nose; and the strongly rolled *r* (represented by '*rr*' in our pronunciation guides). The symbol '*zh*' sounds like the 's' in 'pleasure'. Keeping these points in mind and reading the pronunciation guides as if they were English, you'll be understood just fine. The stressed syllables are indicated with italics. To enhance your trip with a phrasebook, visit lonelyplanet.com.

Basics

Hello.
Olá.   o·*laa*

Goodbye.
Adeus.   a·de·*oosh*

How are you?
Como está?   ko·moo *shtaa*

Fine, and you?
Bem, e você?   beng e vo·*se*

Please.
Por favor.   poor fa·*vor*

Thank you.
Obrigado. (m)   o·bree·*gaa*·doo
Obrigada. (f)   o·bree·*gaa*·da

Excuse me.
Faz favor.   faash fa·*vor*

Sorry.
Desculpe.   desh·*kool*·pe

Yes./No.
Sim./Não.   seeng/nowng

I don't understand.
Não entendo.   nowng eng·*teng*·doo

Do you speak English?
Fala inglês?   faa·la eeng·*glesh*

Eating & Drinking

..., please.   *..., por favor.*   ..., poor fa·*vor*

A coffee   *Um café*   oong ka·*fe*

A table for two   *Uma mesa para duas pessoas*   oo·ma me·za pa·ra oo·ash pe·so·ash

Two beers   *Dois cervejas*   doysh ser·*ve*·zhash

I'm a vegetarian.
Eu sou vegetariano/ vegetariana. (m/f)   e·oo soh ve·zhe·a·ree·a·noo/ ve·zhe·a·ree·a·na

Cheers!
Saúde!   sa·oo·de

That was delicious!
Isto estava delicioso.   eesh·too *shtaa*·va de·lee·see·o·zoo

The bill, please.
A conta, por favor.   a *kong*·ta poor fa·*vor*

Shopping

I'd like to buy ...
Queria comprar ...   ke·*ree*·a kong·*praar* ...

I'm just looking.
Estou só a ver.   shtoh so a ver

How much is it?

Quanto custa?	kwang·too koosh·ta

It's too expensive.

Está muito caro.	shtaa mweeng·too kaa·roo

Can you lower the price?

Pode baixar o preço?	po·de bai·shaar oo pre·soo

Emergencies

Help!

Socorro!	soo·ko·rroo

Call a doctor!

Chame um médico!	shaa·me oong me·dee·koo

Call the police!

Chame a polícia!	shaa·me a poo·lee·sya

I'm sick.

Estou doente.	shtoh doo·eng·te

I'm lost.

Estou perdido. (m)	shtoh per·dee·doo
Estou perdida. (f)	shtoh per·dee·da

Where's the toilet?

Onde é a casa de de banho?	ong·de e a kaa·za ba·nyoo

Time & Numbers

What time is it?

Que horas são?	kee o·rash sowng

It's (10) o'clock.

São (dez) horas.	sowng (desh) o·rash

Half past (10).

(Dez) e meia.	(desh) e may·a

morning	manhã	ma·nyang
afternoon	tarde	taar·de
evening	noite	noy·te

yesterday	ontem	ong·teng
today	hoje	o·zhe
tomorrow	amanhã	aa·ma·nyang
1	um	oong
2	dois	doysh
3	três	tresh
4	quatro	kwaa·troo
5	cinco	seeng·koo
6	seis	saysh
7	sete	se·te
8	oito	oy·too
9	nove	no·ve
10	dez	desh

Transport & Directions

Where's ...?

Onde é ...?	ong·de e ...

What's the address?

Qual é o endereço?	kwaal e oo eng·de·re·soo

Can you show me (on the map)?

Pode-me mostrar (no mapa)?	po·de·me moosh·traar (noo maa·pa)

When's the next bus?

Quando é que sai o próximo autocarro?	kwang·doo e ke sai oo pro·see·moo ow·to·kaa·rroo

I want to go to ...

Queria ir a ...	ke·ree·a eer a ...

Does it stop at ...?

Pára em ...?	paa·ra eng ...

Please stop here.

Por favor pare aqui.	poor fa·vor paa·re a·kee

Behind the Scenes

Send Us Your Feedback

We love to hear from travellers – your comments help make our books better. We read every word, and we guarantee that your feedback goes straight to the authors. Visit **lonelyplanet.com/contact** to submit your updates and suggestions.

Note: We may edit, reproduce and incorporate your comments in Lonely Planet products such as guidebooks, websites and digital products, so let us know if you are happy to have your name acknowledged. For a copy of our privacy policy visit **lonelyplanet.com/legal**.

Sandra's Thanks

A heartfelt thanks to Kate Chapman, Mani Ramaswamy and Kate Mathews for working with me to bring out the best in Lisbon and to each *lisboeta* who assisted me with on-the-ground research while opening their hearts about the city they call home.

Joana's Thanks

To Inês Matos Andrade, Natacha Tonisso and Chitra Stern for sharing their valuable time with me and revealing their local tips. To my parents, for passing me a sense of adventure, and my partner Nick for lending me his ear when I'm writing about my endless travels.

Acknowledgements

Cover photograph: Funicular in Bairro Alto, Lisbon; Benny Marty/ Shutterstock ©

This Book

This sixth edition of Lonely Planet's *Pocket Lisbon* guidebook was researched and written by Sandra Henriques and Joana Taborda. The previous edition was curated by Regis St Louis and written and researched by Kevin Raub. This guidebook was produced by the following:

Commissioning Editor
Kate Chapman

Coordinating Editor
Mani Ramaswamy

Product Editor
Kate Mathews

Senior Cartographer
Julie Sheridan

Book Designer
Virginia Moreno

Assisting Editors
Imogen Bannister, Victoria Harrison, Etty Payne,

Cover Researcher
Gwen Cotter

Index

See also separate subindexes for:
Eating p158
Drinking p159
Entertainment p159
Shopping p159

Sights 000
Map Pages **000**

Sights 000
Map Pages **000**

Our Writers

Sandra Henriques

Baixa & Rossio; Alfama, Castelo & Graça; Marquês de Pombal, Rato & Saldanha Sandra is a Portuguese freelance writer born in the Azores Islands, based in Lisbon for 20+ years. On her travels, she seeks local culture and connects with people and their (always inspiring) stories, even if that means skipping most of the must-see attractions. When she's not writing about travel, culture, and the people she meets in between, she's crafting blood-curdling horror stories in Portuguese. Sandra also wrote the Plan Your Trip chapters for this guide.

Joana Taborda

Bairro Alto & Chiado; Belém; Parque das Nações; Estrela, Lapa & Alcântara Born and raised in Lisbon, Joana has had a thirst for traveling ever since her parents took her on her first flight abroad to Paris. These days, she works as a travel writer and unofficial craft beer taster splitting her time between the Portuguese capital and the semi-tropical island of Madeira. She enjoys finding the hidden stories behind places and connecting with local artisans wherever she goes, preferably with a craft beer in hand.

Published by Lonely Planet Global Limited
CRN 554153
6th edition – April 2023
ISBN 978 1 83869 402 9
© Lonely Planet 2023   Photographs © as indicated 2023
10 9 8 7 6 5 4 3 2
Printed in China